Laurel Moglen

111 Places
in Los Angeles
That You Must
Not Miss

Photographs by Lyudmila Zotova

emons:

© Emons Verlag GmbH
All rights reserved
All photos © Lyudmila Zotova, except:
Boone Children's Gallery (p. 31) – Photo © Museum Associates/LACMA;
Kayaking on LA River (p. 123) – LA River Kayak Safari;
L.A. Derby Dolls (p. 125) – Photo by Marc Campos, L.A. Derby Dolls;
Machine Project (p. 133, top image) – Photo of Josh Beckman's *Sea Nymph*
courtesy of Machine Project; Museum of Broken Relationships (p. 141) –
Courtesy of the Museum of Broken Relationships;
Norton Simon Museum (p. 157) – Norton Simon Art Foundation;
The Source Restaurant (p. 195, top image) – The Source Family after
morning meditation, photo by Isis Aquarian courtesy of Isis Aquarian
Source Archives; Wildlife Waystation (p. 227) – Photo by Billy V Vaughn,
Wildlife Waystation
Art credits: Machine Project (p. 133, top image) – *Sea Nymph* by the artist
Josh Beckman; Velveteria (p. 217) – artwork pictured reprinted
by permission of the artists: Caren Anderson (Liberace in blue vest);
Caren Anderson & Cenon (center Liberace); Jennifer Kenworth
aka Juanita's Velvets (Liberace with red cape); CeCe Rodriguez
(poodle in square frame, left of center Liberace)
© Cover icon Montage: iStockphoto.com/bebecom98, iStockphoto.com/Davel5957
Design: Eva Kraskes, based on a design
by Lübbeke | Naumann | Thoben
Edited by Katrina Fried
Maps: altancicek.design, www.altancicek.de
Printing and binding: B.O.S.S Medien GmbH, Goch
Printed in Germany 2016
ISBN 978-3-95451-884-5
First edition

Did you enjoy it? Do you want more?
Join us in uncovering new places around the world on:
www.111places.com

Foreword

Dear Los Angeles,

So often you are misunderstood, viewed by the world through the narrow lenses of the media and outsiders. Their images portray a fame-obsessed metropolis filled with beautiful people in scenic locations wearing seriously curated wardrobes. There's also the traffic of course, so thick at times, drivers may as well turn their ignitions off. But we devoted Angelenos know that much more is going on outside of the picture frame. Beneath your gridlock and glitzy veneer lies a marvelously sprawling city filled with experiences diverse, strange, titillating, nutritious, and imperfect.

We know you as a place of opportunity; of big dreams, searing disappointments, and painful ideals. A city where the wild meshes with the urban, the beautiful with the ugly, the magical with the real. Brimming with surprises, you offer access to wildly contrasting places and experiences: a club where Mexican drag queens lip sync to 1970s hits, a punk-rock DIY perfume lab, a museum housing the collection of the real Indiana Jones – and always close by is a hike on a chaparral-scented trail.

And the people! Angelenos speak 224 different languages and come from more than 140 countries. You harbor deep thinkers and innovators, contributing to the world cutting-edge art and architecture, scientific advancements, and brave new ideas. To explore your deepest secrets we hung out with surfers, rock climbers, niche collectors, two-steppers, artists, and historians – all of whom helped us discover and divulge the rich and unexpected tales and locales disclosed within these pages.

Sweet LA, this book is our humble attempt to celebrate your depth and complexity. You're the city so many love to hate, and hate to love. But we know the explorers who read this authentic chronicle will, like us, come to adore you, and that means all of you.

– Laurel Moglen & Julia Posey

111 Places

1 The 2nd Street Tunnel

Basking in the glow of traffic

Philip K. Dick fans, get your *Blade Runner* on and see something truly beautiful by entering the 2nd Street Tunnel in the evening at Figueroa Street and heading east. Watch the red reflections of brake lights illuminate the rainbow-shaped tunnel in a glittering spectacle. In the movie, solitary replicant hunter Rick Deckard drives through the tunnel awash in blue hues, the entrance and exits dripping with the constant acid rain of the futuristic city of Los Angeles.

Although Deckard is a loner, he's not alone. The white tiles that line the 2nd Street Tunnel and the ability to easily cordon off the area to traffic and lookie-loos have made it a favorite location for car commercials and fashion shoots as well as other films like the notable sci-fi cousins *Terminator* and *Gattica*. The tunnel may be one of the most filmed unknown icons in Los Angeles. And it almost didn't happen.

Construction began on the 2nd Street Tunnel in 1916. Downtown Los Angeles wasn't the cluster of emerald skyscrapers it is today. It was Bunker Hill, primarily a residential wealthy suburb of opulent Victorian mansions, which separated Downtown from the rest of Los Angeles. That is, until the tunnel came through. The signature white tiles were sourced from Germany and as anti-German sentiment during World War I grew, so did opposition to using a German product. But the architect of the tunnel stood his aesthetic ground and the tunnel was completed, Teutonic tiles and all. Ironically, many of the wealthy inhabitants of the Bunker Hill enclave began to leave the area as the war came to an end and urbanism encroached on their formerly suburban lifestyle.

Many of the Victorians were later partitioned into apartments, two of which became home to writer John Fante and artist Leo Politi (see p. 126), who both went on to champion the new working class of Bunker Hill in their work.

Address 2nd Street between Figueroa and Hill Streets, Los Angeles, CA 90012 (enter by car from Figueroa Street heading east toward Hill Street for the best view) | Hours Always open. Reflections are most dazzling from dusk to dawn. | Tip The Blue Ribbon Garden atop nearby Disney Concert Hall (111 South Grand Avenue, Los Angeles, CA 90012) is almost an acre of tranquility amid the business of Downtown. Enter via the stairs on Grand Avenue near 2nd Street.

2___Adams Pack Station
"Haulin' ass since 1936"

In the foothills where Sierra Madre, Arcadia, and Monrovia meet, the Adams Pack Station in Chantry Flat has been providing asses, as in pack mules, since 1936, and cold beer and other sundries since 1953, to Angeles National Forest hikers and the 81 recreational cabins (serving as private vacation residences) that populate the area around and leading to Sturtevant Camp.

A walk in Big Santa Anita Canyon is like stepping back in time. Trails of varying difficulty start from the Adams Pack Station parking lot. A 3.8-mile round-trip hike past some of the cabins to Sturtevant Falls will make the bottle of icy suds awaiting your return feel like a well-deserved reward. The rustic cottages that dot the trails near Chantry Flat were built between 1907 and 1936 with materials carried in by mules and humans. The cabins exist on a special use permit from the U.S. Forest Service and cabin owners lease the land upon which the dwellings sit.

For those looking to spend the night, primitive campsites at Hoegee and Spruce Grove Campgrounds, about a two- and four-mile hike, respectively, from Chantry Flat, operate on a first-come-first-serve basis. If that seems too hardy, Adams Pack Station's proprietress, Deb Burgess, recently acquired Sturtevant Camp. The nostalgic mountain resort offers cabins for rent on the weekends with flushable toilets and hot showers (learn more at www.sturtevantcamp.com). All food and supplies must be brought in. Make arrangements at least a week in advance with Adams Pack Station to have a mule do the heavy lifting.

Friday to Sunday, the station grills hot food on outdoor barbecues next to the main building, offering excellent burgers and fries and sometimes pulled-pork sandwiches. Live music is performed on Sundays from noon to 5:30pm. Get to the station by 8am on Friday morning for the best chance of seeing the mule team head out on their weekly canyon haul.

Address One Chantry Flat Road, Arcadia, CA 91024, Tel +1 626.447.7356, www.adamspackstation.com, dburgess@adamspackstation.com | **Parking** On-site lot and street parking along Chantry Flat Road. Adventure Pass required for parking. Passes can be purchased at Adams Pack Station or at other adventure retailers. | **Hours** Fri–Sun 7am–5pm | **Tip** Like camping? Millard Campground (4041 Chaney Trail, Altadena, CA 91001) is like a mini-Big Santa Anita Canyon with fewer recreational cabins. A handful of sites sits next to a small stream. No potable water.

3__Amèrica Tropical
A long-lost triumph rediscovered

In the late 1960s, just as the Chicano political movement was establishing its identity, hints of a mural were found bleeding through a whitewashed wall just off Olvera Street in Los Angeles. Originally created in 1932 by revered Mexican muralist and activist David Alfaro Siqueiros, the painting's discovery was perfectly timed. Siqueiros, along with artists Diego Rivera and Josè Clemente Orozco, had become an inspiration for the then burgeoning Chicano art movement.

Siqueiros had been commissioned to create an image of America as the land of plenty. But the artist had other plans. *Amèrica Tropical* depicts two soldiers in the Mexican Revolution aiming at an American eagle sitting atop a double cross on which a Mexican Indian is being crucified. The painting was an enraged criticism of United States oppression and immediately sparked controversy. About a month after his shocking mural was unveiled, Siqueiros was deported from the United States. Within a year, the work was completely covered over. Later, Siqueiros said he'd never intended to paint "a continent of happy men, surrounded by palms and parrots, where the fruit voluntarily detached itself to fall into the mouths of the happy mortals." It's said he often painted at night to keep his artistic choices secret.

Effective protection, not restoration, of the mural began in the 1990s by the Getty Conservation Institute. It took more than 20 years to clean and preserve the discovery. The choice to restore was rejected because experts believed the original colors and artist's hand would be impossible to duplicate.

The mural can be viewed from a rooftop landing quite a distance away. Still, it's profound to gaze upon, especially knowing its history. The building beneath houses the Amèrica Tropical Interpretive Center. It's full of interactive features with rich insight into the times, Siqueiros, and his nearly forgotten masterpiece.

Address Amèrica Tropical Interpretive Center, 125 Paseo De La Plaza, Los Angeles, CA 90012, Tel +1 213.485.6855 | **Public transport** Any means of public transit to Union Station; the center is across the street. | **Parking** Paid lots and metered street parking | **Hours** Tue–Sun 10am–3pm; admission is free | Tip Explore the Art Deco-era Los Angeles Central Library (630 W 5th Street, Los Angeles, CA 90071), which has a gorgeous rotunda ceiling and a children's reading room that's been restored to its original splendor.

4__Angelus Temple
Step right up to hear a tale both wondrous and true

Showman. Preacher. Charlatan. Healer. Aimee Semple McPherson is tough to define. Today, most Angelenos have never heard her name, but it was quite a different story in the 1920s. Her popularity at one point was so great that 10 percent of Los Angeles belonged to her Angelus Temple, which she designed with her mother in 1923.

Widowed at age 19, McPherson remarried at 22. Her call to preach was so strong, she got her start broadcasting sermons through a loudspeaker from the back of her "gospel car," touring up and down the Eastern seaboard with her two children as passengers and her mother at the wheel. Outrageous behavior for a woman in those days. Like any good showman, she traveled, set up tents, held boisterous sermons, and inspired "speaking in tongues." As her fame grew, so did her bank account, and she soon made her way to Los Angeles. Her philosophy focused on the rapture that comes from serving God rather than the torment suffered for forsaking Him. When preaching, she told relatable anecdotes with a permanent smile, a girlish giggle, and down-to-earth humor. Sometimes she spiced up her sermons with theatrics – like when she rode a motorcycle down the church aisle. Apparently she spent bank on Parisian gowns and kept her dyed-blond hair fashionably styled.

After she purportedly healed a wheelchair-bound woman, word of her faith-healing powers spread exponentially. She was the first woman granted a broadcast license from the FCC and the first to preach on the radio. She purchased the radio station KFSG and aired sermons and programs directly from the temple, leveraging the then-modern medium to reach millions.

But along the rise to stardom were also scandals: a kidnapping; a disappearance; and a walk, Jesus-style, through a Mexican desert. There were nervous breakdowns, a falling-out with her daughter and mother, and finally an accidental fatal overdose, in 1944.

Address 1100 Glendale Boulevard, Los Angeles, CA 90026, Tel +1 213.816.1109, www.angelustemple.org, info@angelustemple.org | Parking Metered and unmetered street parking | Hours Sermons: Sun 9:30 & 11:30; Thu 7pm. Be advised that some proselytizing will likely take place. | Tip Keeping up the religious theme, cruise over to the Cathedral of Our Lady of the Angels (555 W Temple Street, Los Angeles, CA 90012) and absorb the airy interior featuring fresco-like tapestries depicting saints standing with anonymous people from around the world.

5 Audubon Center

Into the wild

The Audubon Center is a hidden gem on the northwest tip of the 282-acre Debs Park. This little-known park delivers a gorgeous outdoor experience without the crowds. Don't expect to find conventional swing sets or jungle gyms. Here, nature is the playground. Decomposed granite trails connect to reveal a hand-operated water pump. A small man-made pond holds frogs, which careful hands are welcome to catch, observe, and release. Small buckets and shovels are available for young adventurers to dig and play with. Three solar-powered fountains are home to fish and native riparian plants in an expansive courtyard. Dashing bright blue iridescent damselflies dip and sip in the water. Alert eyes can watch them bend into a C-shape, ovipositor protruding as they lay eggs. Native plants, many propagated on-site, flourish in a wild but well-maintained garden.

Created in 2003, the Audubon Center creatively brought environmental education to an underserved area. Outreach programs, day camps, musical performances, outdoor movie screenings, and of course bird walks, are all part of what the center has to offer.

The airy conference building with taxidermied bird specimens displayed on upper shelves is the first completely off-the-grid government building in Los Angeles. Solar panels supply enough energy to run the entire building, bathrooms, and accompanying fountains. Recycling and reuse is a theme: even the rebar in the concrete structure was made from melted-down handguns.

Although open to all ages, the center is especially good for young families: the complex and gardens are fenced off, allowing little explorers to roam without entering the surrounding parkland.

Feeling more adventurous? A .25-mile trail into the park starts at the far side of the courtyard. It is an easy hike but with a slight elevation that might challenge a child accordingly – and perhaps facilitate an early nap.

Address Audubon Center at Debs Park, 4700 N Griffin Avenue, Los Angeles, CA 90031, Tel +1 323.221.2255, www.debspark.audubon.org, debspark@aubudon.org | Public transport Gold Line to Southwest Museum Station, then a .5-mile walk | Parking Free on-site lot and unmetered street parking | Hours Tue–Sat 9am–5pm, closed Sun & Mon except for special events | Tip Erica Dakings's gluten-free and vegan restaurant, Kitchen Mouse (5904 N Figueroa Street, Los Angeles, CA 90042), is one of the reasons why Highland Park is worth the hype. The breakfast "sausage" is beyond delicious.

6 __ Baldwin Hills Scenic Overlook

A different point of view

The relatively small mountain between Culver City and Baldwin Hills offers a spectacular 360-degree view of the city and an opportunity for a great workout or leisurely stroll, depending on your intent and ambition.

The California State Park attracts many exercise-focused individuals and groups sporting Lycra outfits, more than a few eschewing earbuds to share their workout soundtrack with the masses. The draw is the stacked concrete steps ascending 719 feet with different-height risers. Stair goers often hug and rightfully congratulate one another at the top. Alternatively, a 2.5-mile trail offers a winding route to the summit, or you can simply drive to the upper parking lot.

If the climb doesn't take your breath away, the view, unlike any other in the city, will. To the northeast, Downtown Los Angeles's skyline rises like a cluster of princess-cut emeralds. Moving your eyes past Griffith Observatory and the Hollywood sign, you spot the big blue Pacific Design Center building sitting in the middle of the vista, and to the left the towering buildings on Sunset Boulevard, then Westwood farther west, and Malibu in the distance. To the southwest, LAX busily traffics a steady stream of jets coming and going. The Inglewood oil fields to the south look like a picture from the 1920s, with pumps like oversized Dippy Birds eternally bowing and rising.

The 58-acre park has been reclaimed from oil drilling, and the restoration of native plants, prickly pear cactus, and sunflower bush fosters a healthy home for towhees, bushtits, butterflies, and more. Open on Saturdays, a nature center at the crest of the hill features hands-on exhibits and a theater screening wildlife-related short documentaries. Bathrooms and water are available but no food for purchase, though there is a picnic table for those who bring their own.

Address 6300 Hetzler Road, Culver City, CA 90232, Tel +1 310.558.5547, www.parks.ca.gov/?page_id=22790, info@parks.ca.gov | **Parking** Paid on-site lots and metered street parking | **Hours** Daily 8am–sunset | **Tip** Take a stroll through the Village Green National Historic Landmark (bordered by Rodeo Road, Coliseum Street, Hauser Boulevard, and S Sycamore Avenue), a charming, parklike modernist condominium complex built in 1942 with tree-lined pathways between the units.

7__Berendo Stairs to the Griffith Observatory

Stairway to the stars

The Berendo Stairs, built in 1924 – the same year as the Frank Lloyd Wright Ennis House in the neighborhood – exhibit a bit of the old glamour of Los Angeles. The three flights of steps with graceful sloped concrete banisters ascend 557 feet. Curved benches situated along the way are useful for hikers wanting to take a stylish breather while enjoying the great view. The "neighborhood Stairmaster" ends with a trail into Griffith Park and access to Griffith Observatory.

The logistics: starting at Berendo Street and Crowell Avenue, climb the first and longest set of steps up to Bonvue Avenue. Turn right and follow Bonvue Avenue past the first flight of stairs on the left (this flight lands on Glencairn Road and, although pretty, won't get you to the Observatory without taking a mazelike path through neighborhood streets and skipping the other flights of stairs completely). Continue to the second set of steps on the left, Glendower Stairs, a few feet before Glendower Avenue. The first flight of Glendower Stairs opens to Bryn Mawr Road. Take a quick right and then left to catch the second flight up to Glendower Avenue. Exit the stairs to the right and walk northeast to Glendower Road. The big yellow sign saying "No access to Griffith Observatory" means no access to vehicles – bipeds and quadrupeds (leashed dogs) are welcome.

For hikers wishing to adventure on to Griffith Observatory – and the steps where James Dean famously screamed, "I got the bullets!" in *Rebel Without a Cause* – follow Glendower Road, taking the trail into the park before the road turns sharply right. Head along the trail, staying to the left at the fork. Turn left on the big fire trail road and then take a hairpin turn to the right to reach the observatory. The hike to the observatory from the trailhead is just over a half mile.

Address The intersection of Berendo Street and Cromwell Avenue, Los Angeles, CA 90027 | Parking Unmetered street parking | Hours Always open; however, please use discretion and respect the neighborhood, honoring quiet times. | Tip Trails Cafe (2333 Fern Dell Drive, Los Angeles, CA 90068) has outdoor seating on picnic benches and tree stumps, simple eats, and Stumptown Coffee in the gorgeous setting of Griffith Park.

8__ Biddy Mason Memorial
From slave to wealthy landowner

Despite Biddy Mason's relative obscurity, there is a pocket park with descriptive plaques dedicated to her memory – for good reason. Mason was born into slavery on a Mississippi plantation in 1818. Her master decided to move west in 1847, stopping in Utah for a time before ultimately settling in Los Angeles in 1851. It's said Mason was forced to walk almost 2,000 miles. Along the way, she prepared meals, acted as midwife, cared for her three young daughters, and herded animals.

Mason befriended members of the small African-American community in LA, who probably informed her that California was a free state. But the law pertaining to slaves brought in by their master was unclear, and the specter of the Fugitive Slave Act of 1850 meant that an African American could still be determined a slave at any time and ripped away to a slave state.

To avoid the possibility of losing his slaves, Mason's master decided to return to the South. En route, his ploy was foiled. It's likely a friend of Mason's alerted the sheriff, who showed up in the middle of the night, taking Mason and her fellow slaves to jail – thinking that was the safest place for them. This led to a court trial during which Mason sought and won her freedom as well as the freedom of 13 fellow slaves.

Working as a nurse and midwife, Mason went on to bring babies into the world for all ethnicities and economic classes. She prudently saved her earnings and for $250 bought land on the quiet outskirts of a rough Los Angeles, where the Biddy Mason Memorial is today. The area evolved into a booming business district. A few more keen real-estate moves made Mason a wealthy woman. She shared her prosperity and gave generously. After a devastating flood in 1884, she told the neighborhood grocer she would pay for the food of those who had lost their homes in the storm. Her financial worth when she died was the equivalent of $6 million today.

Address 333 S Spring Street, Los Angeles, CA 90013 | Public transport Purple or Red Line to Pershing Square Station; memorial is two blocks away | Parking Paid lots and metered street parking | Hours Always viewable | Tip Take a peek next door into the iconic Bradbury Building (304 S Broadway, Los Angeles, CA 90013), the sunlight-infused late-19th-century office building where many well-known movies have been shot, including *Blade Runner* and *Chinatown*.

1900   1896

Los Angeles mourns and reveres Grandma Mason.

9 Bluewhale

Hitting all the right notes

We know Hollywood has a reputation for prioritizing image above anything down-to-earth or "real." But that pretense won't fly at Bluewhale, the music club headed up by Joon Lee, a jazz-singing college dropout from South Korea. He was busing tables in New York City and studying to be an architect, when he was struck still by the sounds of Chick Corea and Bobby McFerrin. That's all it took to inspire him to quit school, move to California, and find a voice teacher.

Some say jazz is dead, especially in Los Angeles, where the majority of jazz bands seem to be trying to recapture the past. Bluewhale rejects such staid choices. Lee carefully curates the acts he books with up-and-comers and cutting-edgers, from local to international artists. The space is minimalist; the vibe is earnest. There is no stage, so musicians can set up anywhere, creating an atmosphere of intimacy. Club-goers sit on moveable chairs or leather cubes, allowing listeners to design their own space. Giant canvas slabs hanging from the ceiling are inscribed with thought-provoking quotes from Hafiz, Rumi, and Leon Shenandoah. The demographic is eclectic: 20- to 60-somethings. All these elements brilliantly combine to forcibly quit any possible inclination towards self-consciousness, uniting people for the only thing that matters here: the music.

If providence prevails, you'll visit on a night when the performance is as electric as it was when Brandon Coleman's band played (Coleman is the keyboardist for Alicia Keyes). Coleman's music shattered the room into an explosion of notes and exuberance and *play*. It was as if the band had sex with the audience, slowly leading the crowd to a booming, raucous crescendo (possibly multiple times if you count the solos), inspiring people to jump to their feet, dancing and whooping. All that for a 15-buck cover. Chances are, when you go, you'll get lucky too.

Address 123 Astronaut E S Onizuka Street, Suite 301, Los Angeles, CA 90012, Tel +1 213.620.0908, www.bluewhalemusic.com, info@bluewhalemusic.com | Public transport Metro Gold Line to Little Tokyo / Arts District station, then a .4-mile walk | Parking Paid lots and metered street parking | Hours Daily, doors open at 8pm, music starts at 9pm; closed first Sun of the month | Tip Go early and check out the Geffen Contemporary at MOCA (152 N Central Avenue, Los Angeles, CA 90012). Renovated by Frank Gehry, the museum often hosts challenging and cutting-edge exhibits.

10__ The Bob Baker Marionette Theater

The art of pulling strings

In 1932, eight-year-old Bob Baker saw a puppet show of the nursery rhyme "Jack Sprat" at the once-venerable Bullock's department store on Wilshire Boulevard. Baker was instantly hooked, and returned to see the show several times. The performance errors were what interested him the most – it fascinated him to glimpse the mechanics behind the magic.

Baker soon began training as a puppeteer and by high school, he was building his own marionettes and selling them around the world. After graduating, he worked extensively in animation, which led to a friendship with Walt Disney, for whom he created puppets of Mickey and his pals for the newly opened Disneyland. His puppets were also featured in many well-known movies, including *A Star is Born*, *Bedknobs and Broomstricks, Star Trek,* and *Close Encounters of the Third Kind.* Baker died in 1975, but 3,000 of his handmade puppets live on at the Bob Baker Marionette Theater. Opened in 1962, it is the oldest puppet theater in America. Each puppet is meticulously designed, existing as a specific character for a specific story, strung to perform the necessary behavior. One of Baker's most famous shows, *Balloon Clown*, features "Pierre le Feu," who grabs on to an air-filled orb. As Pierre floats up, the whimsical music crescendos, until his ride pops, and he plummets to the ground, weeping.

During each performance, the theater remains dark while the dolls are spotlit. The puppeteers, dressed in black, are meant to disappear, allowing the marionettes to have full focus. But, it's irresistible to glance up at the earnest faces of the puppet masters dancing with their muses. In fact, observing the delicate manipulation of the marionettes creates a charming lack of illusion. The sincerity and wonder of it all offers a welcome respite from the modern world of screens and emojis.

Address 1345 W 1st Street, Los Angeles, CA 90026, Tel +1 213.250.9995, www.bobbakermarionettes.com, bobbakermarionettes@gmail.com | Parking Paid lot; metered and unmetered street parking | Hours Performance times and dates vary; check website for details. | Tip Around the corner is the tidy Vista Hermosa Natural Park (100 N Toluca Street, Los Angeles, CA 90026), 10.5 acres of trails and meadows, with a view of Downtown LA rising in the background. Please stay alert to the potential realities of an urban park.

11 Boone Children's Gallery

Where anyone can make their mark

You will not see bright primary colors and chunky spill-proof furniture, characteristics one might expect of a family-oriented art space, at the Boone Gallery in LACMA. Instead, visitors walk into a capacious room bedecked with giant windows bursting with natural light. Thick, minimalist, wooden rectangular tables, worthy of a fine, rustic dining room, invite you to have a seat on their sturdy benches. Upon each table are familiar art supplies, like paper, pens, and colored pencils. But also provided are the fixings for making *sumi-e* art. Any workspace that places fat ink markers next to Japanese art materials sends the message of inclusiveness with a total absence of art snobbery.

Sumi-e in Japanese means "ink painting." In this 2000-year-old art form, ink or paint is applied to paper with a bamboo brush made with animal hair. The stiffness of the hair is specially suited to creating images of bamboo or orchid leaves. Boone sets visitors up with brushes, water, and cakes of tempera paint in an array of non-primary (nontoxic!) colors. (The choice of washable paint is the one age-appropriate concession made for the youngsters.) Artists dip their brush into the water, stroke it across the multihued blocks and begin. There's no instruction or pressure here. Those trying their hand at *sumi-e* can free flow or refer to any one of the technique books on a nearby shelf.

Whether perfecting a leaf or drawing stick figures, there's a happy sense of community thrust upon strangers as they share paint and paper, and that's the point. The Boone Gallery seeks to foster many connections – between people, between people and their art, and between people and the art and artists on display at the museum. The paint dries quickly and you get to take your creations home. All ages are welcome. That means adults without children too. All one needs to bring is a willingness to make a mark.

Address LACMA, 5905 Wilshire Boulevard, Los Angeles, CA 90036, Tel +1 323.857.6010, www.lacma.org/kids-families | Parking Paid on-site lots and metered street parking | Hours Mon–Fri 11am–5pm, Sat–Sun 10am–5pm, closed Wed; admission is free | Tip Walk across the street and check out the Craft and Folk Art Museum (5814 Wilshire Boulevard, Los Angeles, CA 90036), cofounded by artist Edith R. Wyle, actor Noah Wyle's grandmother. Longtime Angelenos will remember the days when the museum was still a commercial gallery and beloved cafe called the Egg and the Eye.

12 Brady Bunch House

Here's the story of a house called Brady

Sherwood Schwartz, the late creator of the 1970s television series *The Brady Bunch*, chose the house at 11222 Dilling Street supposedly because he felt it looked like the home of an architect, the occupation of the fictional Brady patriarch. The Studio City residence would somehow hold a family, and that's the way it became the Brady front.

The Dilling house was used only for exterior shots, however. The Bradys' early-1970s kitchen with rust-colored countertops and avocado-green appliances, the iconic floating staircase, and the rest of the interior were created on Stage 5 in Paramount Studios. The single-story Dilling house, built in 1959, didn't match up with the two-story soundstage interior, so a faux window was temporarily added to the left to give the appearance of a second floor, filmed, and then removed. The same exterior shots were used like stock footage throughout the five years that the series aired.

The house last sold in 1979 for $61,000, according to Zillow.com. Current estimates bring the value up to almost $2 million. Not a bad investment. The house's facade looks pretty much the same as it did during its brief close-up. The owners have added a low, gated fence around the property to keep Brady fans at bay, many of whom would take the liberty of walking up the front steps or even audaciously peeking in the window or knocking on the door. Don't let that be you. Respect the privacy of the owner. It's not the same house on the inside anyway. Television is about creating illusions.

Popular as it became, it was only in syndication that the series about the blended family of eight gained the fan base and loyal audience that eluded *The Brady Bunch* during its original run, from 1969 to 1974.

The eternal question remains, if Mr. Brady was an architect, why didn't he design an additional bathroom? Six kids sharing one bathroom? Crazy making.

Address 11222 Dilling Street, Studio City, CA 91602 | Public transport Red Line to Universal City/Studio City Station, then a .7-mile walk | Parking Best as a drive-by, but unmetered street parking available | Hours Viewable from the street only; private residence, not open to the public. | Tip Drive-by a mid-century architectural classic, Raphael Soriano's El Paradiso (11468 Dona Cecilia Drive, Studio City, CA 91604), built in 1964 out of aluminum and glass for an aluminum mogul and his wife. Soriano had the foresight to include three bathrooms. Mr. Brady, are you listening?

13 Bukowski's Bungalow
Home of a dirty old man

The famous underground poet and writer – and legendary drinker – Charles Bukowski rented this humble bungalow for nearly a decade starting in 1962. For years Bukowski had struggled in the literary world, writing short stories and poems without much success, but it was here in 1971 that Bukowski became a novelist. In less than a month, he penned his first book, *Post Office*, about his years as a postal carrier and clerk, a job he quit while living in the De Longpre bungalow, after his editor, John Martin, convinced him to focus full-time on writing. Concerned about covering his living expenses without a regular income, Bukowski made a list of necessities – beer, cigarettes, child support, sundry items – totaling $100 per month, and Martin promised to foot the bill in perpetuity.

The rest is history. But Los Angeles has never been all that great about preserving history, particularly when it comes to architecture. In 2007, the bungalows on the lot, suffering from years of delayed maintenance, were put up for sale and were strong candidates for demolition and new construction. Bukowski fans rallied, and in true Bukowski style, a young office temp and photographer named Lauren Everett built a coalition with Esotouric bus tour founder and historian Richard Schave to defeat the redevelopment Goliaths. Together they convinced the city council to declare the bungalow a designated Los Angeles Historic-Cultural Monument, enabling it to join the ranks of the iconic Hollywood sign and Grauman's Chinese Theatre.

Now, Bukowski fans can drive or walk by his former home and see a hard-earned plaque that commemorates the writer and protects the building from the wrecking ball. Pick up a beer at the Pink Elephant on Western, Bukowski's local liquor store, and raise a toast to the man who once said, "We are here to drink beer. We are here to kill war. We are here to laugh at the odds and live our lives so well that Death will tremble to take us."

Address 5124 De Longpre Avenue, Los Angeles, CA 90037 | **Public transport** Red Line to Vermont/Sunset Station, then a .7-mile walk | **Parking** Unmetered street parking | **Hours** Viewable from the street only; private residence, not open to the public. | **Tip** Zankou Chicken (5065 Sunset Boulevard, Los Angeles, CA 90027), just a block away, spit roasts a mouth-watering chicken with a sublime garlic butter sauce. The tangy tabbouleh tastes like Mediterranean heaven.

14__Bulgarini Gelato
A taste of Rome in LA

Roman-born Leo Bulgarini calls himself a terrible businessman. His gelato is relatively expensive. He offers only a dozen carefully curated flavors at a time. Use of preservatives is out of the question. But what might be bad for the bottom line is transcendent for the palate. Lucky is he who stumbles upon Bulgarini's nondescript storefront.

You don't need a discriminating palate to sense deep in your soul that a bite of this frozen delicacy is like eating a mouthful of wonder. Why? Because Bulgarini cares deeply enough to use real ingredients of the highest quality and takes lots of time to create his sorbets and gelato. Macerated plum peels are cured for five to six days before being transformed into an intensely flavored sorbet that tastes like plum times ten. In the summer, there might be four varieties of peach available, each one made with a different type of the fruit. For the pistachio gelato, only Sicilian nuts are used. Bulgarini mashes them into a thick, mossy-green-colored butter, and *that* is what you're consuming with every lick of the dense, rich, sweet chilled confection. His macadamia-nut gelato? He travels to Hawaii once a year and visits a farmer who dries his nuts with a standard room fan. Bulgarini says it's the only way to ensure that no mold grows on the nuts.

When he and his wife were touring Europe for two years learning how to make pastries, they visited Sicily. There, Bulgarini found that the gelato at all the shops tasted the same because most of the essential flavors were premade by a company and preserved with citric acid. Influenced by his restaurant-owning uncle, who crafted three delicious gelatos by hand, for Bulgarini there was no other option but to take the hard way out.

The location of this hidden treasure, in a seemingly deserted strip mall in a non-touristy area of the city, makes the discovery of it that much more miraculous.

Address 749 E Altadena Drive, Altadena, CA 91001, Tel +1 626.791.6174, www.bulgarinigelato.com, info@bulgarinigelato.com | **Parking** Free on-site lot | **Hours** Wed–Thu 12pm–10pm, Fri 11am–11:30pm, Sat 10am–11:30pm, Sun 12pm–10pm | **Tip** A visit to Bulgarini is a fitting reward for completing the nearby hike to the ruins of the Echo Mountain Resort (see p. 68).

15__ The Bunny Museum

Hare hoarding

It all started with a nickname. Candace Frazee called the love of her life "honey bunny," and Steve Lubanski, the object of her affections, liked it. In fact, he was so taken, on their first Valentine's Day together, he gave her a plush bunny. Then, for their first Easter, she gave him a porcelain bunny. Not wanting to wait for the next holiday, Steve started giving Candace a bunny every single day. Within five years, they had amassed 7,000 rabbit-themed items. By 2016, that number had spiked to over 32,000.

Since 2011, the museum has held the Guinness World Record for the largest collection of rabbit-related objects. There are also about a dozen live Thumpers happily hopping around the place. One of them is a Flemish giant, unique for its huge size.

Shopping for bunny paraphernalia is a passion for the love buns. They find their treasures at secondhand boutiques, swap meets, and gift shops – especially during post-Easter sales. One gem was discovered at the Goodwill thrift-store chain. Steve picked up a plush bunny and laid down a quarter for it. Little did he know what a steal he had sniffed out. It was a Gund – a famously expensive and collectible German brand of stuffed animals. When he checked later, its value was a comparatively prodigious $85.

Frazee welcomes visitors warmly, leading them from room to room, enthusiastically sharing stories and background about the collection. The entry corridor is lined with glass cabinets crowded with porcelain cottontails. Sneak a peek into the private hallway, and you might glimpse a tower of packaged toilet paper featuring bunny graphics. The overflowing house has fuzzy creatures smashed into every possible crevice, eliciting both bafflement and wonder. Even the yard features a gigantic rabbit topiary.

Want to know the "hoppy" couple's favorite object? Their lips are sealed – that would be like picking a favorite child!

Address 1933 Jefferson Drive, Pasadena, CA 91104, Tel +1 626.798.8848, www.thebunnymuseum.com, sila88@aol.com | Parking Unmetered street parking | Hours Daily, by appointment only; $5 suggested donation | Tip Go for a hike at nearby Eaton Canyon (1750 N Altadena Drive, Pasadena, CA 91107). Try the trail to the waterfall, about 1.5 miles from the Eaton Canyon Nature Center.

16_ California Institute of Abnormalarts

Gaffs! Wonders! Truth! Illusion!

Carl Crew, a former mortician and the owner of Abnormalarts, a nightclub and sideshow collection, is a showman at heart. Donning a top hat, he will delight in leading you through his miniature reproduction of San Francisco's Chinatown, regaling you with tales. Glowing red paper lanterns hang from above, and cabinets full of curios line the pathway. His connection to Chinatown goes back to childhood. As a boy on his walk to school, Crew would regularly pick up fried wontons there, and subsequently forged tight bonds with the locals. Apparently he became so trusted, they bestowed upon him dead, embalmed members of their families.

You can view two such mummies, encased in glass. There's Fat Choy, described by Crew as a magician who performed in opium dens, assisted by his pet monkey. Then there's Madame Wong, a dwarf who Crew says was not just a magician, but also a thief. While performing, she would release opium smoke through two black dragon heads. Audience members, lulled into a stupor, were then relieved of their valuables. Take note of her "Thai fingernail" – a long, pointy tool worn over a fingertip – used to remove rings from unsuspecting patrons.

In another cabinet, straight from Scotland, is the Hand of Glory, said to be the shriveled paw of a burglar. Legend has it that such metacarpus were once used by thieves to rob homes. The scalawags would enter, plead for a place to rest for the night, and light the disembodied digits like candles. Those slumbering in the house were said to fall into a charmed sleep, allowing the tricksters to steal their treasures.

Beyond the corridor of creepiness is a patio where kitschy old TV and film clips play. In the main room, performers stage a freak-oriented variety show. "We're maximalists here – not minimalists," explains Crew. "What's the point, but to be noticed?"

Address 11334 Burbank Boulevard, North Hollywood, CA 91601, Tel +1 818.221.8065, Facebook: California Institute of Abnormalarts | **Parking** Metered and unmetered street parking | **Hours** Tue–Sun 8pm–2am; ticket prices vary per show | **Tip** Just a 5-minute drive away is Norton Sales (7429 Laurel Canyon Boulevard, North Hollywood, CA 91605), a prop shop specializing in aerospace and industrial items since 1962. It's open to the general public too, so anyone with a sci-fi inclination can whir around the store looking for items to make the robot of their dreams.

17 __ Candelas Guitars

Guitar heroes

Three generations of guitar builders stand behind the East Los Angeles institution of Candelas. Known for meticulous handcrafted classical and flamenco guitars, guitarrons, vihuelas, ukuleles, and the colorful sonorous timbre they resonate, Candelas has earned the respect and love of musicians everywhere, including Jose Feliciano, Charo ("Cuchie-cuchie!"), and Los Angeles's own Los Lobos.

The story of Candelas starts humbly, in Torreon, Mexico. Two brothers orphaned in the early 1900s were raised separately but in the same town. One got to go school. The other went to work. Candelario Delgado Flores, known as Candelas, hit the books. Porfirio Delgado Flores ended up with a hammer and entered the carpentry trade. Candelas, a great singer and musician, convinced his brother Porfirio to make a guitar. And so the family luthier legacy launched.

The business grew by word of mouth as more and more musicians discovered the quality of their instruments – delightful to play, like ear candy to hear. The brothers hopscotched from Torreon to Juarez to Tijuana to Los Angeles. They set up shop in Boyle Heights in 1948. At one time, Candelas Guitars swelled to five stores, from Tijuana to Hollywood, but they now centralize all work and sales through the current Boyle Heights location. The shop also offers lessons.

Porfirio's grandson Tomas Delgado is the current face of Candelas and a fantastic guitar player himself. Lucky patrons can hear him testing instruments built by his own talented hands. With such fine craftsmanship, one might expect that only bona fide rich professionals could afford these guitars. Although not cheap, an amateur might augment the purchase of his or her very own instrument by holding a few bake sales or busking in the park. And who knows – with practice, the right location, and a Candelas guitar, one might even move from performing on the streets to the arena stage.

Address 2724 E Cesar Chavez Avenue, Los Angeles, CA 90033, Tel +1 323.261.2011, www.candelas.com, info@candelas.com | Public transport Gold Line to Soto Station, then a .5-mile walk | Parking Metered street parking | Hours Tue–Fri 9am–6pm, Sat 9am–3pm, Sun & Mon closed | Tip Check out Artists & Fleas (647 Mateo Street, Los Angeles, CA 90021), a local vintage and artisan-based flea market located just 2.5 miles southwest of Candelas (open every 3rd weekend of the month, 11am–5pm, www.artistsandfleas.com).

18__Catalina Tile
Chewing gum, red clay, sun, and sea

Despite being only about 22 miles away from the megalopolis of Los Angeles, Catalina feels like, well, an island. The surrounding deep blue and turquoise waters are dotted with bright flashes of orange Garibaldi damselfish. Harbor seals bark and glide through thick kelp forests around moored sailboats and motor yachts. Late chewing-gum magnate William Wrigley was seduced by the island lifestyle, and his purchase of a controlling interest in the Santa Catalina Island Company in 1919 gave him ownership of Catalina, the only developed Channel Island and the central jewel of the corporation.

Ever the business mogul, Wrigley was constantly looking for ways to monetize his investments. He founded Catalina Clay Products Company in 1927 as a way to create employment for local residents. Until 1937, the signature colorful and graphically bold tiles were made from red clay harvested from the island itself. The factory on Pebbly Beach Road was in operation for only a decade, making the original Catalina tile quite rare and valuable. Today, six-inch-square tiles, originally priced at 25 cents, typically sell for $200 to $300 apiece. Downtown Avalon businesses, such as the former Catalina Casino – now a contemporary movie theater – and public fountains are blanketed with them. Crescent Avenue, Avalon's main street, serves as a default open-air museum of Catalina tile and is well worth a leisurely stroll.

The Wrigley Memorial on Avalon Canyon Road, about two miles into the interior of the island, is covered in thousands of hand-painted, primarily blue, Catalina tiles. Wrigley could afford it. The memorial is nestled in the canyon foothills of the Botanic Garden, which also displays the eight plants endemic to Catalina. Shuttles run to the memorial and gardens, or you can rent a golf cart, the island transport of choice, for a self-guided tour.

Address Crescent Avenue, Avalon, CA 90704 & Wrigley Memorial at the Botanic Garden,
1402 Avalon Canyon Road, Avalon, CA 90704, www.catalinaconservancy.org | Getting
there By boat: Catalina Express leaves from San Pedro, Long Beach, and Dana Point. See
www.catalinaexpress.com for schedule and fares. | Hours Crescent Avenue: always open.
Botanic Garden: daily 8am–5pm; admission: $7 adults, $5 seniors & veterans, $3 children
& students. | Tip Bookend the day with coffee in the morning and beer or wine at night at
Catalina Island Brew House (417 Crescent Avenue, Avalon, CA 90704).

19 The Charlie Hotel

If only the walls could talk

Hidden behind a wooden gate on a quiet residential street in West Hollywood, a compound of English Tudor-style bungalows has become a fairy-tale-like home away from home for those lucky enough to discover its charms. Sprinkled with the pixie dust of Hollywood history, the property at 819 North Sweetzer was once owned by film legend Charles Spencer Chaplin, infamous for his sexual exploits, and famous for his artistic proliferation. Chaplin built this cluster of cottages after purchasing the land – once a farm owned by actress Ruth Gordon's family – in 1924. Converted into the exclusive Charlie Hotel in 2008, it has played host to a constellation of starlets, both in Chaplin's day and more recent times, from Marlene Dietrich and Marilyn Monroe to Natalie Portman and Liv Tyler. It remains, after all these years, a place of refuge for the beautiful and creative.

One of the residences, a quaint three-story house, once served as Chaplin's workspace and is now named after the diminutive Hollywood icon. Interestingly, the bathroom contains two showers. One is designed to modern standards. The other is preserved in its original state: custom-built to Chaplin's size, it's a perfect fit for anyone under 5'5".

During the period Chaplin worked at the bungalow, he would likely have been making, completing, or conceptualizing some of his most well known and respected movies: *The Gold Rush*, *The Circus*, *Modern Times*, and *City Lights*. The last, a silent film starring Chaplin's famous "Tramp" persona, feels like a defiant move for the artist. Shooting began in 1928, a time when "talkies" were in full-bore production. It's said Chaplin was concerned that giving voice to the Tramp would alienate loyal audiences. However, the advent of sound meant the movie could be scored, and score it he did. It went on to enjoy giant financial success and is considered by many to be Chaplin's most masterful work.

Address 819 N Sweetzer Avenue, West Hollywood, CA 90069, Tel +1 323.988.9000, www.thecharliehotel.com, info@thecharliehotel.com | Parking Unmetered street parking; on-site spaces for hotel guests | Hours Check-in is 3pm–5pm. Casual tours are given to those not staying at the hotel. Please call in advance to reserve a time. | Tip Indulge in a trip to Fred Segal (8100 Melrose Avenue, Los Angeles, CA 90046), a retail compound comprising LA's trendiest boutiques.

20＿CicLAvia

Pedal power

One of the great laments about Los Angeles is its car-centric culture, and that as we travel to and fro in our private vehicles, soundtracks blaring, we fail to experience the city on a human level or make direct connections, unless we happen to literally crash into one another and are forced to exchange phone numbers and insurance information.

CicLAvia, which started on 10.10.10, kicks that paradigm to the curb. Every few months, the cycling activist organization, in partnership with the City of Los Angeles, closes down area streets to car traffic for a day in a select neighborhood. Only bikes, skaters, big wheels, scooters, pedestrians and other non-motorized modes of transport are allowed to traverse the streets. Area businesses, food trucks, dance troupes, artists, and musicians, not to mention cyclists, all contribute to make the day uniquely stellar.

The average bike pace at CicLAvia is at least a third slower than a car would travel on those same streets. Walking takes it down to about 3 mph. Neighborhoods that previously registered as a blur open up into vibrant public spaces with restaurants and shops, spotted with CicLAvia pop-ups like the Mobile Mural Lab, a panel van that serves as a canvas. Paints provided.

Traversing Los Angeles streets without the hazards of motorists grants you the opportunity to look up, feel the wind on your face, and be surrounded by other people doing the same. What might you see? Tall bikes, with their Frankenstein-like double frames, seem to abound at CicLAvia, as do dogs in baskets and sidecars. Stop at one of the many hubs for a chilled beverage, some food, or a hands-on seminar by LA Metro on how to load your ride onto a city bus bike rack.

Whether it be Wilshire Boulevard, the Valley, or the Southeast Cities, each CicLAvia is an opportunity to experience a different part of this complex, sprawling metropolis at its best.

Address Locations throughout Los Angeles; see website for upcoming event details; Tel +1 213.355.8500, www.ciclavia.org, info@ciclavia.org | Public transport Every CicLAvia route includes at least one Metro train station, often more. | Hours 9am–4pm on event days | Tip Located in the former garage of famed supercharger Distaso Automotive and Dynamometers Specialists, Coco's Variety (2427 Riverside Drive, Los Angeles, CA 90039) is an eclectic bicycle retailer and repair shop offering quality new and used bikes ("faded champions reborn for another chance at glory").

21__Cindy's Diner

Site of the original cheeseburger

While cooking up a plain burger one day, 16-year-old Lionel Stern-berger spontaneously decided to do something no one had ever done before: he added a slice of cheese on top, because, well, it seemed like a good idea. The year was approximately 1924 and young Lionel had unwittingly just invented what would become one of America's most beloved and classic dishes: the cheeseburger.

The story goes that, at the time, Lionel was working at his family's roadside fruit, tobacco, and hamburger stand, which later became their restaurant, Rite Spot. Rite Spot opened in the late 1920s or early 1930s and featured "The Aristocratic Burger: The Original Hamburger with Cheese" for a cool 15 cents. An old photograph shows the setup as simply a long outdoor countertop with an awning and no walls – California roadside dining on what was then part of historic Route 66.

Today, the location is occupied by Cindy's Diner. Ownership of Cindy's has changed hands several times since the eatery opened in 1948. In 2014, new proprietors and trained chefs Paul Rosenbluh and Monique King took over and respectfully updated the kitchen, but left the wonderful electric-orange Naugahyde booths and counter seats untouched. Starburst wallpaper adorns the walls. It's circa 2010, but that's okay, because it feels so midcentury appropriate. The Googie signage is refreshingly nonflamboyant, and was restored through a Kickstarter campaign. Patrons can easily transport themselves back to the early 1960s while savoring chicken-fried mushrooms and washing them down with a root-beer float. It's high-end diner food with a Southern spin. Everything is made fresh on the premises; the freezer is barely used.

And yes, there is still a cheeseburger on the menu, but in a sign of the changing times, today Cindy's specialty is their veggie burger – the menu features a different one every week.

Address 1500 Colorado Boulevard, Los Angeles, CA 90041, Tel +1.323.257.7375, www.cindyseaglerock.com, info@cindyseaglerock.com | **Parking** Free on-site lot | **Hours** Tue–Sun 7am–10pm, closed Mon | **Tip** Justin Timberlake's music video "Can't Stop the Feeling" was shot at Cindy's. In fact, the diner's signage is the opening shot. Sit in the same booth as Timberlake did – it's the first one to the right of the entrance.

22 Clifton's Cafeteria

An homage to kitsch and kindness

In 1935, the United States was reeling from the Great Depression and many Americans were poverty-stricken and hungry. That's when Clifford Clinton founded Clifton's Brookdale Cafeteria in Los Angeles, the second in a chain of what would become a dozen themed eateries. He was a Bay Area boy whose father and grandfather were in the restaurant industry. But Clinton wasn't just a restaurateur; a man of charity, he was driven to help the poor. Clifton's Cafeteria was guided by the ethos "No guest need go hungry for lack of funds." During the restaurant's first three months of business, Clinton gave away 10,000 lunches for free. His generosity nearly sank him into bankruptcy.

Current owner Andrew Meieran tries to stay true to the spirit of Clinton's compassion. His hope is to employ people from local shelters, like the Midnight Mission, who have received training in food and hospitality. The challenge is how to support these workers as they achieve success. It's an honorable goal in progress.

Meieran spent millions renovating the restaurant over five years. Remaining loyal to Clifton's original interior design, he carefully restored the first floor to its 1930s appearance, evoking a sense of being enveloped in the redwood forests of Santa Cruz, where Clinton once hunted. A giant fake redwood extends from the second through fourth floors. The walls adjacent to the sequoia on all three levels have seamless murals of trees painted on them.

Also on the first floor is the beloved tiny two-seat chapel. The diorama within it fell into disrepair, but under Meieran's guidance now depicts mountains blanketed with trees. A recorded voice once intoned within the shrine: "If you stand very still in the turmoil of life, and you wait for the voice from within, you'll be led down the quiet ways of wisdom and peace, in a mad world of chaos and din."

Address 648 S Broadway, Los Angeles, CA 90014, Tel +1 213.627.1673, www.cliftonsla.com | Public transport Purple and Red Lines to Pershing Square Station, then a .3-mile walk | Parking Paid lots and metered street parking | Hours Cafeteria: Mon–Fri 11am–9pm, Sat-Sun 10am–9pm; Monarch Bar: daily 11am–2am; Gothic Bar: daily 6pm–2am | Tip It's just a 10-minute walk to the famous Millennium Biltmore Hotel (506 S Grand Avenue, Los Angeles, CA 90071), where the Academy Awards were held in the 1930s. An afternoon tea in the Rendevous Court is a wonderful way to experience the hotel's history and grandeur.

23_Corita Art Center
Nun with a mission

Her work is held in the Museum of Fine Arts, Boston, and New York's Whitney and Metropolitan museums, among others, and she is considered a Pop Art contemporary of Andy Warhol. Her bright silkscreens and watercolors challenged poverty, hunger, racism, and the war in Vietnam, all the while unironically embracing love. Artist, activist, and nun – yes, nun – Sister Corita Kent (1918–1986) began her art career in Los Angeles while in the order Sisters of the Immaculate Heart of Mary, an order that became known for its counterculture values in the 1960s.

Sister Corita, a beloved teacher from 1947 on, ran the art department at Immaculate Heart College from 1964 to 1968, now the campus of the American Film Institute. She was known for pushing her students to move beyond their perceived limits and embrace their creative spirits. She organized a lecture series for her students called Great Men, inviting artists of all kinds, including John Cage, Buckminster Fuller, Alfred Hitchcock, and the dynamic design duo Ray and Charles Eames to share their thoughts, theories, life experiences, and work practices.

Corita Art Center is located in an unassuming building on the campus of Immaculate Heart High School. It's more a long hallway lined with Kent's framed artworks than a gallery proper, with an additional room that holds a collection of prints in flat files. Make an appointment in advance to view the works in the archives, some of which are available for purchase; prices range from $200 to just under $3,000 for an original. A list of prints for sale can be found in the Corita Art Center vestibule gift shop.

Sister Corita Kent left the order of the Immaculate Heart of Mary in 1968. The majority of the sisters were to follow two years later, when their effort to reform their charter, which included shedding their wool habits, was denied by the Archbishop of Los Angeles.

Address Immaculate Heart High School, 5515 Franklin Avenue, Los Angeles, CA 90028, Tel +1 323.450.4650, www.corita.org, info@corita.org | **Parking** Free parking on exercise field. Enter via the American Film Institute parking entrance on Franklin, then continue 30 feet to high-school parking kiosk. Security will direct you. | **Hours** Mon–Fri 10am–4pm | **Tip** The hike to Bronson Caves (3200 Canyon Drive, Los Angeles, CA 90068), in nearby Griffith Park, is an easy quarter mile. The man-made caves were used in many films and television shows, most notably as Adam West's "Bat Cave" for the 1960s TV series *Batman*.

24__The Cowboy Palace Saloon

Where honky-tonk and horses still reign

Open the door of the Cowboy Palace Saloon, and you immediately find yourself standing on the edge of a well-trodden wooden dance floor. And if it's Thursday night at 7pm, you'll see before you about 20 women kicking up their heels in perfect unison. Synchronized grapevines and Monterey turns are executed at an impressively fast pace. Leading the dancers is a surefooted Marie Del Giorgio, a country-western dance teacher at the saloon for 26 years.

The Cowboy Palace Saloon has been around since the 1970s. The crowd is loyal. Susie, a middle-aged woman with long blond hair and clad in a plaid shirt and cowboy boots, was looking for something new when she signed up for a line-dancing class here. That was 12 years ago; she's been coming three times a week ever since. More than dancing (which she says is better than going to the gym), the classes led Susie to meet a whole new circle of girlfriends – and her current boyfriend.

The community is tight; the walls offer a safe place, a real home away from home. Funerals, weddings, birthday parties, and marriage proposals are common occurrences at the Cowboy Palace. During the week, the demographic skews over 55. On the weekend, the crowd is more eclectic, including hipsters, bikers, college students, and all sorts of ethnicities and races.

The walls are draped with three American flags and laden with horsey quips, photographs, ropes, and saddles. Worn-out cowboy boots are strung together and hung off the side of the bar. There are a couple of pool tables. There is no cover charge and dance classes are free. Live music roars nightly. On Sundays, you will likely see a horse or two hitched to the post out front.

Back on the dance floor, it's showtime. Marie shouts out, "No tags! No restarts!" The ladies all yell, "Yippee!" and the music begins.

Address 21635 Devonshire Street,Chatsworth, CA 91311, Tel +1 844.426.9725, www.thecowboypalacesaloon.com, info@cowboypalace.com | **Parking** Unmetered street parking | **Hours** Daily 3pm–2am; live music at 8:30pm on Mon, Wed, Thu; 9pm on Fri & Sat; 6pm on Sun | **Tip** Devour some delicious soul food four blocks away at Les Sisters Southern Kitchen & BBQ (21818 Devonshire Street, Chatsworth, CA 91311), which serves up classic down-home dishes like southern fried chicken and collard greens.

25 Demonstration Gardens at Theodore Payne

Go native!

For any native of California, or a naturalized Californian, little vexes more than the decrying of the lack of seasons. P'shaw! Head out into the wild and you'll see the beauty of the changing seasons, subtle to be sure, but present all the same. Summer brings long, arid days with the crisp smell of sun-warmed soil as the native plants hibernate. Fall typically blazes in with hot Santa Ana winds before mellowing to cooler temperatures. In a good year, winter rains plump up the flora and tantalize the nose with the satisfying scent of wet earth. And then comes spring, when the brown landscape explodes into a show of wildflowers: orange poppies, purple lupines, and the red blossoms of the well-named firecracker penstemon. And where to best see this in action? The Theodore Payne Foundation, in the canyons of Sunland.

Theodore Payne was a British expatriate brought up in the Victorian horticulturist tradition, which involved painstaking plant pressings, Latin identification of plants, and pretty hand-lettered herbariums documenting it all. Young Theodore Payne, parentless by 12, immigrated to the United States at the age of 21, stepping off the SS *New York* to pen his occupation in the ledger at Ellis Island as "Seed Trade." He headed straight for Los Angeles and spent hours outdoors exploring the wild canyons, accessible year-round thanks to the mild seasons. He fell in love with the native plants and considered them California's greatest asset.

The Theodore Payne Foundation demonstration gardens honor his legacy by growing a living catalog of the exquisite and well-adapted plants of the region, including the *Lupinus paynei*, which Payne identified as a new species. Plants and seeds are available for purchase through the foundation's retail nursery, but the delicious scent of native chaparral is free.

Address Theodore Payne Foundation, 10459 Tuxford Street, Sun Valley, CA 91352, Tel +1 818.768.1802, www.theodorepayne.org, info@theodorepayne.org | Parking Free on-site lot | Hours Nov–June, Tue–Sat 8:30am–4:30pm, closed Sun & Mon; July–Oct, Thu–Sat 8:30am–4:30pm, closed Sun–Wed | Tip Hike the Wildflower Trail north of the nursery and keep an eye out and ear cocked for the abundant California quail in the area hills.

26 Descanso's Ancient Forest
The land before flowers

Phone calls steadily stream into Descanso Gardens; lots of people wish to drop off plants they no longer want or can care for. Most of the florae aren't the right fit for the botanical garden. But one rare day in December 2014, a man called with an offer Descanso couldn't refuse; a collection of cycads, ten years in the making.

Cycads are ancient plants whose origins reach back in time, predating flowers, to an era when dinosaurs walked the Earth. In fact, cycads have survived 200 million years of changing circumstances, prevailing under wildly different climatic and geologic conditions. They grow very slowly, which makes for their long life span. When a climatic emergency hits, a plant embryo can go dormant for a long time, then "wake up" once the danger has passed. Cycads have minimal requirements for thriving; they don't use a lot of water, and compost makes them happy.

Most plants have male and female parts on them – but not the cycads. They reproduce by their cones. Male and female cones are quite different by size, shape, and color. Sporophylls, woody modified leaves on the cones, bear the sexual parts. The male cone produces blobs of pollen covered with hairs that wiggle, each the size of a pinpoint – thus visible to the naked eye – large for a plant. The female cone has ovules, which, when fertilized, develop into seeds.

That fateful call in 2014 led to an infusion of cycads at Descanso. About 170 plants and 66 species are thoughtfully planted by native region – Africa, Asia, Madagascar, Australia, and Mexico – in a garden called the Ancient Forest. At first glance, the cycad might appear to be a fern or palm, but they are related to neither. Some featured in the gardens no longer exist in the wild; humans, the cycad's biggest threat, are recklessly harvesting them. Descanso is doing its part to allow the otherwise hearty plant to do what it does best: endure.

Address Descanso Gardens, 1418 Descanso Drive, La Cañada Flintridge, CA 91011, Tel +1 818.949.4200, www.descansogardens.org | Parking Free on-site lot | Hours Daily 9am–5pm; $10 general admission | Tip Devour what's thought to be some of the best Mexican food in Los Angeles at nearby La Cabañita (3445 N Verdugo Road, Glendale, CA 91208). The salsa is so good, it's drinkable.

27 — Discovery Room at the NHM

Don't just look – touch

Originally housed in the Dodgers VIP lounge, the towering stuffed polar bear that now stands in the second-floor Discovery Room at the Natural History Museum of Los Angeles was donated by the baseball organization "for the enjoyment of children" – according to the worn brass plaque at the bear's feet. And enjoyed it has been. Unlike most museum exhibits, visitors are welcome – even encouraged – to touch the furry mammal. The bear, rearing up on its hind legs, is a little worse for wear thanks to the many fingers that have lovingly stroked it over the years.

The polar bear is just one of many unexpected "hands-on" experiences offered by the museum, which first opened its doors in 1913. Almost a century later, it underwent an extensive renovation and reinvigoration of the traditional natural history museum model. The north side of the campus opens to a 3.5-acre urban wilderness garden full of native plants and official "get dirty" areas. Patrons are invited to dig through compost and discover what lives in the soil. Inside the museum, Dinosaur Encounters vividly brings to life the infamous Tyrannosaurus rex and Triceratops. Puppeteers wear elaborate costumes designed by the same artists who created the dinosaurs for the movie *Jurassic Park*. The realistic-looking puppets stalk the North American Mammal Hall with blinking eyes and attention-grabbing growls, demonstrating the perceived hunting habits of the late Cretaceous beasts.

On the first Friday of the month from February through June, the Natural History Museum morphs after hours into what may be LA's coolest nightclub. The diorama halls are recast as a performance space for bands and a bar that features a live DJ and illuminated coffee tables and sofas. First Fridays admission is $18 to $20 for non-members and free for members, but tickets must be reserved in advance.

Address 900 Exposition Boulevard, Los Angeles, CA 90007, Tel +1 213.763.DINO, www.nhm.org, info@nhm.org | **Public transport** Expo Line to Expo/Vermont Station, then a .2-mile walk | **Parking** Paid lots and metered street parking | **Hours** Daily 9:30am–5pm. Admission: $12 adults, $9 students & seniors, $5 kids ages 3–12. | **Tip** The Space Shuttle Endeavor made a dramatic entrance when it was flown into LAX on the back of a 747 and was towed via city streets to its new home at the neighboring California Science Center (700 Exposition Park Drive, Los Angeles, CA 90007).

28 Drum Barracks
Civil War Museum
When camels roamed the west

The proposal to use camels to explore the Southwest was kicked around by the burgeoning United States congress for about 19 years before being approved in 1855. The government agreed to allocate $30,000 to purchase 34 camels from Egypt and Turkey and transport them to Texas. They imported two types of camel, the dromedary – one-humped, light, swift, and often trained for riding and racing; and the Bactrian – two-humped, heavier, slower, and able to carry hundreds of pounds on its back.

Camels are an ancient species, thought to have existed for more than 5,000 years. Known to be hardy, powerful, and fast, they were relied upon for food and transportation by desert dwellers, who considered the animal sacred and even treated them like family members. Able to understand many human commands and words, they are intelligent and loyal – if treated with respect. Treated badly, camels will retaliate. This was the unfortunate experience of the Texas-based soldiers, who were left to care for the regal beasts when the camel experts were sent to battle in the Civil War. The camels' perceived stubbornness led the ignorant men to kick, whip, and pummel them. The retribution typically dished out by the animals came in the form of a well-aimed giant spit-wad – actually vomit.

It was 1862, Year Two of the Civil War, when the camels were unloaded in Wilmington, where they remained for about 18 months, mostly sleeping and eating. Ultimately, they were let loose in the desert, eventually perishing.

The Civil War museum is intimate, consisting of seven exhibition rooms, including a corner devoted to the ill-fated camel experiment. The building is the last remaining structure of the 22 that once comprised the westernmost outpost of the Civil War.

Address 1052 N Banning Boulevard, Wilmington, CA 90744, Tel +1 310.548.7509,
www.drumbarracks.org | **Parking** Free on-site lot | **Hours** Tours: Tue, Wed & Thu
10am & 11:30am, Sat & Sun 11:30am & 1pm, closed Mon & Fri. There are no self-guided
tours $5 suggested donation. | **Tip** Phineas Banning, one of the founders of Wilmington and
a fervent supporter of the Union, donated land for the Drum Barracks fort to be built. Take
a tour of his carefully restored 23-room residence, built in 1864, now the Banning Museum
(401 E M Street, Los Angeles, CA 90744).

29__The Dude's Bungalow

"Does this place look like I'm married?"

Iconic movies about Los Angeles abound – Billy Wilder's *Sunset Boulevard*, John Singleton's *Boyz in the Hood*, John Houston's *Chinatown* all capture quintessential elements of the city – and right up there in the pantheon of celluloid depictions is the Coen brothers' cult classic, *The Big Lebowski*. *The Big Lebowski* is a fantastic and ridiculous tale of mistaken identity, stolen money, pornography, bowling, and the triumph of the deadbeat bum.

A few blocks north of Abbot Kinney Boulevard and east of Venice Boulevard, the bungalow complex where the character Jeffrey Lewbowski – we're talking about the Dude here – lived. The interior shots were filmed on a soundstage in West Hollywood. The then humble bungalow on Venezia Avenue was used for exterior scenes. Picture the night shot at the end of the opening montage, as a bathrobe clad, bowling-ball-toting Dude traipses through the courtyard with his bag of groceries before he enters his place and his troubles begin. Or the scene where the awkward landlord solicits the Dude on the steps outside his bungalow for notes on his upcoming dance recital and a late rent check.

Venezia Avenue at Zeno Place, just south of the bungalow, appears in the film too. The fed-up Dude, fresh from helping his special lady friend, confronts private eye Da Fino, a brother shamus, who has been trailing him in his blue VW bug for days.

The Big Lebowski fans – rich ones at least – had a chance to purchase the Venice property when the bungalow was put up for sale in 2011. The Dude's place sold for $1.59 million, rug not included. The new owners were no lightweights and gave the property a good scrub and upgrade. The Dude, even with Maude's compensation, would have been priced out.

Refrain from indulging your inner nihilist and storming the property or walking down the pathway. This is a private residence, man. Please check it out from the street only.

Address 606 & 608 Venezia Avenue, Venice, CA 90291 | Parking Best as a drive-by, but unmetered street parking available | Hours Viewable from the street only; private residence, do not enter the property. | Tip Grab an oat soda at the Hiano Cafe (15 W Washington Boulevard, Venice, CA 90292), a Venice institution since 1969. Hiano serves beer and wine only – sorry, dude, no White Russians.

30__Echo Mountain Resort

Los Angeles has ruins too! Seriously, it does!

Atop Mount Lowe, with a magnificent 360-degree view of the San Gabriel Valley, once flourished the now long forgotten turn-of-the-20th-century Echo Mountain Resort. On this six-mile hike to and from the resort's ruins, you'll wander by remnants of the funicular that once carried visitors up the side of the mountain. At the summit, pieces of foundation are mostly all that remain for hikers to explore. There's an excellent photo display depicting the resort in its glorious heyday.

Climbing to the ruins requires hikers to navigate a switchback for 2.5 miles on a clearly marked path that is rustic at best. That is, lots of rocks litter the four-foot-wide trail, and at times you briefly walk alongside a sheer drop, with zero vegetation lining the edge, and no guardrail. On a clear day, the view is extraordinary; you can see all the way to Catalina Island.

That view – and the healthful environment of the "White City" – drew people to the world-class resort. From 1893 to 1938, the Mount Lowe railway ascended the side of the mountain at a breathtakingly steep angle. Once at the top, visitors were struck by the sight of the bright white Echo Mountain House. The cozy wood-paneled lobby was graced with a piano and fireplace. The hotel had 70 sleeping rooms and rose to four stories. Around the grounds, guests could enjoy a tennis court, dance hall, small zoo, mule rides, an observatory, and a searchlight so powerful it illuminated homes in the valley below.

In 1900, a fire leveled the hotel. The observatory remained open to visitors until 1928, when powerful winds blew off the top. The Alpine Tavern, built close by, also burned down, 36 years later. By 1938, White City was no more. The visionary behind it, the once extremely wealthy inventor Thaddeus Lowe, died penniless in his daughter's home, after sinking his entire fortune into his castle in the sky.

Address Sam Merrill Trailhead, Altadena, CA 91001; trailhead begins where Lake Avenue dead-ends at East Loma Alta Drive, at the entrance to the Cobb Estate | Parking Unmetered street parking | Hours Daily, sunrise to sunset | Tip Check out the Pasadena Museum of California Art (490 E Union Street, Pasadena, CA 91101). Its focus on the Golden State's artists, architects, and designers helps bring California's unique contributions to light.

31 Echo Park Lake
A heartwarming tale of stealing the right thing

By Los Angeles standards, Echo Park Lake is old. Completed in 1870 as a reservoir, it was converted into a recreational lake in 1892. Landscape architect Joseph Henry Tomlinson planted the shores with large swaths of lawn, willows, and California fan palms and designed a pathway that follows the water's edge. Old-timey photos show park visitors throwing a line out in hopes of catching a fish.

By 1920, lotuses had made an appearance in the lake and quickly flourished. In July 1980, the annual Lotus Festival was launched. Over the next few decades, hundreds of thousands of people from around the world came to see the floating blossoms, said to be the biggest display of lotuses on the planet. But by about 2006, the cherished flower was showing signs of decline. In 2008, the *LA Times* reported there were just "twelve tattered leaves" remaining. Many reasons were given to try to explain their heartbreaking disappearance. Few knew that in 2005, a Los Angeles gardener, enchanted by the flowers, had furtively cut off a stalk of tubers and tucked it away in his car.

While many smart people put their heads together to figure out how to bring back the now iconic flower, the thief had propagated his booty successfully and was selling the aquatic plants. Rumor of his lotus mongering got out. He was approached by a representative of the landscaping company charged with restoring the lotuses to the lake. The flower robber fessed up and now, Echo Park Lake has the same blooms it did in 1920. You'll find the thin stalks, at times soaring up to five feet high and topped with thick white and pink petals, stretching out of a carpet of large, cuplike leaves. Spread across the pond, their beauty hits you like a sucker punch.

Today, you can enjoy the lotuses up close by taking a ride on the shimmering lake – which also offers a lovely view of Downtown LA – in a pedal boat, canoe, or gondola.

Address Echo Park, 751 N Echo Park Avenue, Los Angeles, CA 90026,
Tel +1 213.481.8577, www.laparks.org/dos/aquatic/facility/echoParkPaddle.htm | Parking
Paid lot behind Sunset Boulevard between Logan and LeMoyne Streets; unmetered street
parking | Hours Daily 9am – 1/2 hour before sunset; closed Thanksgiving & Christmas |
Tip Stop in to the lakeside cafe, Square One at the Boathouse, for lunch or breakfast and
choose from a family-friendly menu that emphasizes farm-fresh and organic ingredients.

32 Edelweiss Chocolates

Where Lucy's lightbulb lit up

For some time, Lucille Ball had been discussing a scene for *I Love Lucy* in which she switched jobs. She and her team were stuck on which occupation would be appropriate for a 1950s woman. One day, Ball parked in the back of a Beverly Hills chocolate shop and walked through the factory, heading to the front of the store. Along the way, she passed a woman in the assembly line having trouble keeping up. Inspiration struck. The "chocolate scene" in Season Two, Episode 39, in which Lucy and her sidekick Ethel can't wrap the chocolates on a speeding conveyer belt fast enough – forcing them to stuff the confections in their mouths, hair caps, and blouses – is one of the most beloved comedic scenes in sitcom history. The shop that triggered the hilarity? Edelweiss Chocolates.

Just like Ball, you can still park in the back of Edelweiss and walk through the intimate, white-walled factory, witnessing the chocolatiers at work. The rich scent of chocolate hovers in the small rooms filled with white antique candy machines. Cascading folds of melted chocolate drench the centers of the candies as they slowly make their way through an 80-year-old dipping machine. The oldest tool is a hand-cranked nut grinder made in 1896. It's smallish with a design that's elegant, sturdy, and practical.

When crafting their handmade chocolates, Edelweiss considers a host of variables – such as the ratio of shell to filling and the tidiness of the coating and decoration (no streaks or drips allowed). Since 1942, chocolate-covered pretzels have been a specialty. Considered exotic back then, they're one of the most sought-after items at Edelweiss today. The luxurious chocolate enrobes the barely salty, snappy, biscuit-flavored twists – decadent and delicious.

For two and a half weeks, Ball visited the shop daily, absorbing the techniques of candy making. Visitors can schedule a tour and do the same.

Address 444 N Canon Drive, Beverly Hills, CA 90210, Tel +1 888.615.8800, www.edelweisschocolates.com | Parking Free two-hour lots and metered street parking | Hours Mon–Fri 10am–6pm, Sat 10am–5:30pm, closed Sun. Call ahead to arrange a tour of the factory. | Tip Walk over to the Paley Center for Media (465 N Beverly Drive, Beverly Hills, CA 90210), where you can watch or listen to an international collection of more than 160,000 programs, spanning almost 100 years of television and radio history.

33__ The Edison

Like stepping into a glass of whiskey

Eight feet of water greeted Andrew Meieran when he first saw the space that is now the Edison. Yet despite its sorry state, Meieran was intrigued; peeking up through the soggy neglect were hints of the building's industrial past.

In 1877, Thomas Higgins made his fortune when he struck a copper vein in Arizona. He moved to Los Angeles in the early 20th century, determined to construct the most modern building in the city – and he did. Made of concrete, it had elevators, a central vacuum system, a purified water filtration system, and a developing utility called electricity. He built a power plant in the basement six years before Los Angeles installed the city's first power pole (bringing in electricity from Pasadena). Talk about vision undeterred.

More than a century later, Meieran too had vision, when he snapped up the dilapidated subterranean property and turned it into a sprawling serpentine nightclub. Caramel lighting, heavy velvet curtains, hidden rooms, and luxurious leather lounge chairs seduce revelers. Filled with the original boiler and steam and pressure tanks and turbines, the vibe is industrial, romantic, and nostalgic.

Keen explorers should keep an eye out for the easily overlooked. Before you enter the club, peer up at the facade. The building was originally eight stories. At the top of the eighth floor, you'll see white decorative trim – a remnant of where the roof once was. Despite the city's initial resistance, Higgins received approval to add two more stories. Notice the tenth floor has white decorative trim as well.

While the formerly flooded rooms are now dry, walls still weep at the entrance of the Ember Parlour, near the steam tunnel in the Generator Lounge and adjacent to the restrooms. Meieran says it's because there's a hot spring under the building that has its way with the walls, depending on the state of California's drought.

Address 108 W 2nd Street, Los Angeles, CA 90012, Tel +1 213.613.0000, www.edisondowntown.com, info@edisondowntown.com | **Public transport** Gold Line to Union Station, then a .5-mile walk | **Parking** Valet is available at the corner of Harlem Place Alley and 2nd Street; paid lots; metered street parking | **Hours** Wed–Fri 5pm–2am & Sat 7pm–2am | **Tip** Ten minutes away (on foot) is the Last Bookstore (453 S Spring Street, Los Angeles, CA 90013), a sprawling, two-story love letter to bibliophiles. Filled with unique and quirky nooks and spaces, the shop stocks thousands of new and used titles.

34___Egyptian Theatre
Home of the first movie premiere

Although famously known for the Chinese Theatre, Sid Grauman worked his movie palace entrepreneurial magic on the Egyptian Theatre prior to cement-casting the hands and feet of celebrities a block and a half west.

Grauman was recruited by Charles Toberman, a real-estate developer who became known as Mr. Hollywood for his reenvisioning of a wide swath of land he subdivided into what is now Hollywood. Toberman pictured pulling the East Coast entertainment hub – along with the more local downtown Broadway Boulevard, with its spectacular movie palaces – west to Hollywood.

Built in just a year and a half, the Egyptian Theatre capitalized on the public fascination with archaeologist Howard Carter's search for King Tut's tomb. The exterior was painted in Egyptian-style hieroglyphics and the interior was outfitted with a sunburst ceiling featuring a plaster relief of reeds from the Nile River.

The Egyptian opened in October 1922 with the screening of *Robin Hood.* The courtyard served as an open-air lobby and grand entrance to the theater. Fans lined up on one side, with flashbulbs of media cameras going off on the other – and celebrities, including era heartthrob and *Robin Hood* star Douglas Fairbanks, paraded larger than life down the middle, launching the tradition of the Hollywood premiere. Two weeks later, almost as if it were written into the script, Howard Carter opened the sarcophagus of King Tutankhamen after an eight-year quest.

Such a glorious beginning was followed by steady decline and well-intended but harsh remodels to modernize the grand palace. Thankfully, the cinephile cultural institution American Cinematheque acquired the theater in 1996 and reinvigorated the faded Hollywood legend. Movies are screened almost daily, and on select Saturdays, a behind-the-scenes tour of the Egyptian is open to the public.

Address 6712 Hollywood Boulevard, Los Angeles, CA 90028, Tel +1 323.461.2020, www.americancinematheque.com/egyptian/egypt.htm | Parking Paid lots and metered street parking | Hours Tours: 10:30am on select Saturdays. See website for tour dates, admission prices, and a schedule of film screenings. | Tip The former Knickerbocker Hotel (1714 Ivar Avenue, Los Angeles, CA 90028) bears the dubious distinction of having been the place where filmmaker D. W. Griffith died of a cerebral hemorrhage while standing under the lobby chandelier. Peering in from the sidewalk, you can glimpse the chandelier; however, the Knickerbocker is now a retirement home and closed to the public.

35__El Segundo
Butterfly Preserve

A site for winged creatures, great and small

The postage stamp-sized El Segundo Blue butterfly doesn't have it easy. With a life span of just a few days to two weeks, it also holds the dubious honor of being the first insect to be named an endangered species. Adding insult to injury, its primary home is the land surrounding the Los Angeles International Airport. Not exactly the ideal environment for butterflies to flourish – and perhaps an even worse place for humans. That wasn't always the case. In 1928, a popular housing development called Surfridge opened here, just blocks from the beach, offering homes with a view of the sweeping coast next to a modest airfield. That small landing strip would grow to become LAX, the world's third-busiest airport. And Surfridge lay directly beneath the deafening flight path.

Surfridge residents were forced to move, leaving behind a ghost town. But land in LA rarely lies fallow, whether 67 million jets pass above it annually or not. Enter the El Segundo Blue. The petite butterfly's habitat once stretched from Pacific Palisades to Santa Monica, until real-estate development claimed every available acre of shoreline. While undesirable for humans to inhabit, the abandoned Surfridge property was deemed a suitable home for the dwindling population of the El Segundo Blue, which feeds on buckwheat found in coastal dunes.

In 1992 the Surfridge land was converted into a 200-acre preserve to protect the Blue. Today, visitors can walk the fenced perimeter and catch a glimpse of the periwinkle-colored butterflies, which shed their cocoons from mid-June to mid-August and enjoy a very brief summer of love. Females lay their eggs under the leaves, which hatch about a week later. The caterpillar phase lasts about a month, followed by a ten-month cocooning period. When the butterflies emerge, the whole dang process starts all over again.

Address Between Dockweiler Beach and Los Angeles International Airport, El Segundo, CA 90245 | Parking Park near Rindge Avenue and Waterview Street for a quieter walk; metered parking also available on Vista del Mar next to the beach | Hours Always viewable from the walking/bike path surrounding the preserve; interior of the preserve closed to visitors | Tip Visit another nature sanctuary, the Antelope Valley California Poppy Preserve (15101 Lancaster Road, Lancaster, CA 93536), in springtime, when the brown hills erupt with orange poppies. Experience the Musical Road (see p. 148) on your drive to the Poppy Preserve.

36__Evergreen Cemetery
All comers accepted

Established in 1877, the Evergreen Memorial Park is the oldest existing cemetery in Los Angeles. Unique to its history is its willingness to accept all races, ethnicities, and religious affiliations. Armenians, Japanese, Chinese, American Civil War soldiers, and prominent local figures like Isaac Van Nuys, as well as the unknown and the indigent, all share the sprawling resting place.

Among Evergreen's most unusual residents are more than 400 circus performers and carnival workers, buried side by side in the eastern end of the grounds. None of the graves appear fancy, but they are cared for with one fresh flower on each plot. "Showmen's Rest," created by the Pacific Coast Showmen's Association, provided the space for this nomadic crowd of people, who might not have had money for a proper burial and often thought of one another as family.

Buried there is the 38-year-old Daisy Evelyn Marrion, a beautiful aerialist who, during a section of her routine where she was supposed to soar over the crowd secured by ropes tied around her ankles, instead plummeted 80 feet in front of a live audience. The ropes had failed. It's said that watching Marrion free-fall and ricochet off a tree, a trailer, and a wire fence left the spectators in stupefied silence. Remarkably, she held on for six days before her shattered body finally succumbed.

You'll also find the grave of "Dainty Dotty" Jensen. At 585 pounds, Dotty held the title of "Fat Lady" with Ringling Brothers in the 1930s and 1940s. Audiences delighted as she made her flesh jiggle when she laughed. She died prematurely of a heart attack at 43, weighing 350 pounds.

A nearby headstone remembers Hugo Zacchini, the "Human Cannonball." His act was blasting out of a cannon designed by his circus-owning dad. Ironically, despite the risks of his death-defying profession, it was a common stroke that ended his life, at the relatively old age of 77.

Address 204 N Evergreen Avenue, Los Angeles, CA 90033, Tel +1 323.268.6714 | **Parking** Free on-site parking | **Hours** Daily 7am–5pm | **Tip** Fill up on delicious and non-greasy Latin food with lots of vegetarian and vegan options at Un Solo Sol Kitchen (1818 E 1st Street, Los Angeles, CA 90033), about .2 miles from Evergreen.

37__Fast and Furious Home

Living life a quarter mile at a time

The fictional home of Dodge Charger-driving criminal-turned-hero Dominic Toretto, played by Vin Diesel, was shot up by machine-gun-toting, motorcycle-riding Asian gangs and completely blown to bits in *Fast and Furious 7*. Computer animation razed the house, leaving a smoky heap on-screen. In reality, the wooden two-story residence in Angelino Heights still stands.

The house at East Kensington Road was used for filming both exterior and interior scenes. The big backyard with its view of the cinematic downtown skyline sparkled like an equally telegenic co-star behind the party scenes. And the 4,891-square-foot seven-bedroom home provided ample space for the indoor shoots.

What started as a street-racing flick morphed into a quasi-superhero film series with plenty of bulging muscles and cleavage and a good-looking multicultural cast that captured the hearts and fantasies of many. *Fast and Furious* has become Universal Pictures' most lucrative franchise. Its longevity was called into question, however, when *Fast and Furious* star and real-life sports-car enthusiast Paul Walker died in a high-speed crash in 2013. Walker and his racing partner were coming from a charity event in Valencia, north of Los Angeles, when the Porsche they were in clipped a tree and then hit a lamppost, killing Walker and the driver almost instantly. Universal completed *Fast and Furious 7* using already-shot footage of Walker, computer animation, and Walker's brothers as stand-ins.

Fast and Furious fans, minding all traffic laws, of course, can cruise about 3 miles northwest to Silver Lake's steep Micheltorena Street (between Lucile Avenue and Sunset Boulevard), where Walker's character, Brian O'Connor, jumped his ride in fast and furious pursuit of the fleeing motorcycle gang.

Of all the films' farfetched feats, the most improbable is surely finding a traffic-free road in LA for street racing.

Address 722 E Kensington Road, Los Angeles, CA 90069 | Parking Best as a drive-by, but street parking available | Hours Viewable from the street only; private residence, not open to the public. | Tip Neighboring Carroll Avenue (crossroad Edgeware Road, Los Angeles, CA 90026) is considered Los Angeles's first suburb, and in 1983, the city designated the area its first historic district, protecting the Victorian-era homes from demolition and restricting non-period renovations.

38 Fire Pits at Dockweiler Beach

Vanity of the bonfire

The beach bonfire is an age-old tradition that goes back far beyond the days of Gidget, *Beach Blanket Bingo*, and the crooning Beach Boys. Nestled next to a fire, marshmallows on skewers, blankets draped over shoulders, and hands warmed by mugs of hot cocoa, many Southern Californians consider it practically a birthright. But in 2013, the beloved seaside ritual sparked a firestorm of opposition that threatened to end the practice altogether.

A group of beachfront homeowners in Orange County's tony Newport Beach, living downwind of a cluster of fire pits, complained of health hazards linked to diminished air quality caused by the sooty particulate, and demanded the removal of 60 fire rings. Their protests expanded into a SoCal-wide legal battle that affected all beach bonfire areas and played out like a modern-day French Revolution. The proletariat pit fire proponents declared that the proposed ban was a classist effort to shut out the 99 percenters' beach access. The wealthy homeowners cited reports from the South Coast Air Quality Management District to support their claims. After legislation to keep the coastal bonfires open was unanimously approved by the State Assembly in 2014, a compromise was reached out of court to locate the wood-burning fires at least 700 feet away from any private residences.

Dockweiler Beach, just west of LAX, is one of only two beaches in LA that allows for bonfires in designated cement rings (the other is Cabrillo Beach in San Pedro). Arrive early for the best chance of securing a pit. The sites are at a premium on summer weekends and holidays. Only nontreated wood without nails or paint is permitted to burn. Bring a flat grill and camp coffeepot if you want to heat water for hot beverages. Keep in mind, booze is prohibited and citations and fines are issued.

Address Dockweiler Beach, 12000 Vista del Mar, Playa del Rey, CA 90293, www.parks.ca.gov/?page_id=617 | **Parking** Paid beach lots, $6–$13, lots close at 10pm; metered street parking | **Hours** Daily 6am–10pm | **Tip** The Tripel (333 Culver Boulevard, Playa del Rey, CA 90293), just over 3 miles north, rethinks American dining with tantalizing small plates like truffle salted nuts and artisanal house-made pickles. Bigger bites, burgers, salads, and an impressive selection of craft beers and cocktails are on the menu too.

39__Frank Gehry's Residence
Where the master architect makes his bed

It's hard not to chuckle when you walk up to the house where the internationally renowned architect Frank Gehry has lived since 1977. On a humble plot of corner land in beachy Santa Monica, rule-breaking Gehry has built a deconstructionist ramble of an abode that seems to wrap its modern arms around the original Dutch colonial house in a big hug.

Part showcase, part experiment, the structure exudes a devil-may-care insouciance and total rejection of conformity. Random placements of chain-link fencing protrude where you might expect a balcony. There's an unpainted piece of plywood here and there. Sheets of industrial corrugated metal line the exterior walls, which are interrupted by tilted, protruding glass cubes, box-like atriums, juxtaposing opacity and transparency. Long horizontal planks of thick, curved wood are used for fencing, with bits of peek-a-boo holes breaking it up. It seems wonderfully ridiculous, a wink at what Gehry is all about.

Gehry's first big splash came in 1997 with the inauguration of his Guggenheim Bilbao, a modern and contemporary art museum. In 2010, *Vanity Fair* asked 52 leading architects, teachers, critics, and deans of major architecture schools what building they thought was the most aesthetically significant since 1980. More than half cited Guggenheim Bilbao and in general, works by Gehry got the most votes, leading the magazine to call him "the most important architect of our age." The building was trailblazing, taking the world's breath away with its metallic curves and angles. In Los Angeles, he's most famous for the silvery, undulating, chunky, and angular Walt Disney Concert Hall in Downtown LA, completed in 2003.

Back on the Westside, visitors can stand on the sidewalk in the (now) posh Santa Monica neighborhood and easily admire the master's eye-catching clash of shapes and materials.

Address 1002 22nd Street, Santa Monica, CA 90403 | Parking Unmetered street parking |
Hours Viewable from the street only; private residence, not open to the public. | Tip Visit
Brentwood Country Mart (225 26th Street, Santa Monica, CA 90402), an intimate upscale
shopping center where you'll likely catch sight of a celebrity while browsing.

40__Frederick R. Weisman Art Foundation

Home is where the art is

It is a whirlwind of a tour at the Weisman Foundation. For 1.5 hours, a small group of visitors gathers at the former home of Frederick R. Weisman, and is whisked through room after room of the Mediterranean-style mansion. The dazzling array of artwork overflows with modern and contemporary pieces by Kandinsky, Picasso, Giacometti, Miró, Magritte, and Warhol, as well as lesser-known artists. In fact, the eclectic collection is so extensive, some paintings are placed on the ceiling.

Weisman made his mark as a businessman, first at Val Vita Cannery, then at Hunt Foods, where he became president at age 31. In 1970, he became one of the first American distributors of Toyota cars. He used his fortune to make philanthropic contributions as well as buy important works of art, predominantly in the 1980s and early 1990s.

Among the foundation's eight Andy Warhols is an iconic suite of ten big and bold Marilyn Monroes, which hang in the Grand Stair of the Annex building. Roy Lichtensteins abound, including his 1977 *Reclining Nude*. Ed Ruscha's *World and its Onions* is placed prominently in the master suite (hint: look up).

Modernist Willem de Kooning's breakthrough painting, *Pink Angels*, is located to the right of the fireplace in the living room. In contrast and close by is one of his rare black-and-white paintings, *Dark Pond* – pensive and brooding.

Weisman's library includes two life-size figures of his parents by artist Duane Hanson, whose various hyper-realistic sculptures of people are scattered throughout the house.

The passionate collector wanted to share his good fortune in business with the public by inviting people into his home to experience art in a more personal setting.

Address Holmby Hills, Los Angeles, CA 90077, Tel +1.310.277.5321,
www.weismanfoundation.org, tours@weismanfoundation.org | **Parking** Inside gate only; no
street parking allowed | **Hours** Tours by appointment only: Mon–Fri 10:30am & 2pm. Exact
address will be given to guests once they have booked their tour. | **Tip** Visit another grand
estate, Virginia Robinson Gardens (1008 Elden Way, Beverly Hills, CA 90210). Built in
1911, it is one of the first homes in Beverly Hills.

41__Front Porch Farmstand
Family farming in the city

The Dervaes family, father Jules, daughters Anais and Jordanne, and son Justin, run a productive organic backyard farm in northeast suburban Pasadena, a stone's throw from the 210 freeway. Despite their entire property being a fifth of an acre in a standard housing tract, they've dedicated about half their land to their garden, and grow over three tons of produce annually. The literal fruits (and vegetables) of their labor can be bought at the Front Porch Farmstand. The Front Porch also carries fresh baked breads, granola, local honey, canned preserves, and other goods made or harvested by the Dervaes and area artisans.

Paterfamilias Dervaes immigrated to New Zealand from the United States with his young family in 1973. There, he practiced homesteading and beekeeping. Just over a decade later, he came to Pasadena and bought the house that would become their city farm. Over a process of years, the Dervaes family continued to simplify their lives, ousting their dryer for a clothesline, reducing their water consumption, and eventually mulching over their entire front yard to transform it into a productive edible garden with the intent of nourishing their kin. What didn't end up on the kitchen table, Dervaes loaded onto a bike and peddled to area restaurants like the Arroyo Parkway Grill. The demand for quality locally harvested organic produce grew, and so did their business, Urban Homestead.

The farmstand offers fresh organic produce by appointment and a subscription CSA box in partnership with other nearby farms. Seeds are also available for purchase if you'd like to grow your own.

Call and place an order in advance, especially for greens, which can be picked fresh for the customer. Urban Homestead also hosts events ranging from Sunday-night potlucks with live music, aka Hootenannys ($10–$15 suggested donation), and workshops.

WHAT'S GROWING

VEG Swiss CHARD • KALE •
Mustard • SALAD • LETTUCE

SAUTE   Pre Order Only

ARUGULA   HERBS
PEA SHOOTS*   RoseMary
                           Parsley
RADISHES   Sage

Address Urban Homestead, 631 Cypress Avenue, Pasadena, CA 91103,
Tel +1 626.765.5704, www.urbanhomestead.org, info@urbanhomestead.org |
Public transport Gold Line to Memorial Park Station, then a 1-mile walk | **Parking**
Unmetered street parking | **Hours** By appointment only; check website for upcoming
events and workshops at Urban Homestead. | **Tip** Gold Bug (22 E Union Street,
Pasadena, CA 91103) is one of the most interesting stores in Los Angeles County,
run by a father-mother-daughter team that curates a truly eclectic mix of artisan jewelry,
art, select fashion, and taxidermy.

42___Gaam Karaoke
Noreabang until the sun comes up

Dan Sung Sa Plaza, a nondescript strip mall in the northwest quadrant of Berendo and 6th Streets, can serve as a wormhole gateway to an all-inclusive Koreatown experience that includes great food, heavy drink, and a night filled with song. Any part of that equation can be removed or moderated by preference, but excess is a signature motif of *noraebang*, or Korean karaoke.

In the center of the L-shaped, no-nonsense row of shops, a red sign written in Hangul with a hanja sidebar and a Latin alphabet subheader marks Gaam Karaoke. If you don't read Korean, you won't see "Gaam" printed anywhere on the sign, but you will see "karaoke." Gaam Karaoke, not to be confused with Gaam Restaurant two and a half blocks west in Chapman Market Plaza, offers private room rentals, each of which typically features a table in the middle to hold a song book, two wireless mics, a tambourine, upholstered booths, Hite beer bottles, and glasses of Korea's most popular distilled alcohol, soju, served neat. For the uninhibited, tables can double as a dance floor in a pinch. Kpop, Jpop, Chinese, and English song selections are listed by number. Type the number or a favorite title into the remote. Sounds easy, but for added challenge and authenticity, the remote is only in Korean.

Gaam updates its song catalogue about every three to four months, slightly slow for diehard karaoke aficionados, but good enough if you're looking for a way to kick back and have fun with friends. *Noraebang* is best experienced in packs, and splitting an entire bottle of whiskey in your private room is de rigueur.

Weekends can get busy. Best to book a room in advance and confirm the price. Costs will vary based on the time spent singing and the number in your party. Like a comedy club, a drink minimum is typical. Negotiating in Korean has its advantages, as does a smile and a good attitude.

Address 3309 W 6th Street, Los Angeles, CA 90020, Tel +1 213.909.5581 | Public transport Red Line to Wilshire / Vermont Station, then a .3-mile walk | Parking $2 valet; metered and unmetered street parking | Hours Daily 6pm–2am; reservations are highly recommended. | Tip When Roy Choi and Anthony Bourdain crashed Dan Sung Sa, in the same strip mall just two stores away (3317 W 6th Street, Los Angeles, CA 90020), on Bourdain's show *The Layover*, they let out a well-kept secret. The food here is delicious. Cheese corn might be your favorite mistake of the evening.

43 Gower Gulch

Calling all cowboys!

Starting in the 1920s and lasting well into the 1950s, B-western movies were all the rage. Cheap to make and sure to find an audience, it was said a western was made every ten days. Real cowboys, as well as actors dressed as cowboys, used to hang out in full Western regalia – big Stetsons, low-slung belts, chaps, spurs, and often pistols – at the intersection of Gower Street and Sunset Boulevard in hopes of picking up day work on a movie. Casting agents would contact prospective actors on the pay phones in the back of Columbia Drug, formerly on the southeast corner, or swing by and load up a truck of extras to film in the Valley. The area was christened Gower Gulch.

These were rough men, accustomed to living by cowboy laws and working as true range riders. But as the landscape began to change, with the range breaking into homesteads and even subdivisions of the very valley where they filmed, the heyday of cattle runs came to an end. So, many displaced cowboys, in search of a job where riding a horse still mattered, even if it was for a movie, came to Gower Gulch.

Rarely is it wise for coarse men with firearms to sit aimlessly. Quarrels are bound to arise and sharp words can trigger violence. Once at Gower Gulch, when cowboy/actor Johnny Tyke allegedly said to Jerome "Blackjack" Ward, "I'll cut your heart out," Blackjack pulled out his .45 and fatally shot Tyke in the head. Ward was acquitted on the shaky claim of self-defense, even though no weapon was found on Tyke's body. A fellow cowboy actor testified his dog had dug up Tyke's knife in the bushes near the fight. Blackjack later went on to pistol whip a man in a bar with the same gun, unloaded this time.

In the 1970s, the strip mall on the southwest corner of Gower and Sunset was remodeled with a kitschy Western backdrop to pay homage to the legacy of the loitering drugstore cowboys of Gower Gulch.

Address Southwest corner of N Gower Street and Sunset Boulevard, Los Angeles, CA 90028 | Parking Paid on-site lot | Hours Always open | Tip Amoeba Music (6400 Sunset Boulevard, Los Angeles, CA 90028), three blocks west of Gower Gulch, is a great record store with many in-store concerts in an intimate setting.

44__Griffith J. Griffith Statue
Ode to a deranged philanthropist

His wife knelt before him at his demand. He told her to close her eyes. She begged him to put away his gun. Ragingly drunk, he ripped into her, questioning her fidelity and accusing her of conspiring to poison him. She denied any wrongdoing. Then he shot her in the face. She managed to stumble to the hotel window and throw herself out. Miraculously, she survived the fall, landing on the roof below, the impact only breaking her shoulder. The gunshot wound took her right eye and deformed her face.

The husband in this harrowing story is Griffith J. Griffith, who, in 1896, donated 3,015 acres of his Los Feliz property to the City of Los Angeles to be used as a public green: Griffith Park. It was seven years later, on September 3, 1903, that he attacked his wife, Christina (nèe Mesmer) Griffith.

Christina, a devout Roman Catholic and social worker, came from a prominent and wealthy Los Angeles family. Griffith was a farm boy from Wales, raised by various extended family members. In his earlier years he was known as an earnest, hardworking, and charming businessman, who made his fortune in mining and real estate. But people's opinions of Griffith soured with age. Journalists and associates referred to his grotesque gnomelike appearance, and described him as having "delusions of grandeur" and strutting "like a turkey gobbler."

His powerful lawyer argued a defense of "alcoholic insanity" and finagled him a mere two-year sentence for the violent assault on his wife. After serving his time, Griffith returned to LA and spent much of the rest of his life trying, unsuccessfully, to win back the public's respect.

Griffith died in 1919, but you can visit his likeness in the park named after him, where a bronze full-figure statue of the controversial philanthropist by artist Jonathan Bickart was unveiled in 1996.

Address Griffith Park, 4730 Crystal Springs Drive, Los Angeles, CA 90027 (statue is located near the entrance on Los Feliz Blvd), www.laparks.org/dos/parks/griffithpk | **Parking** Free on-site lot at Griffith Park Recreation Center (3648 Los Feliz Boulevard, Los Angeles, CA 90027); unmetered street parking on Riverside Drive | **Hours** Statue always viewable | **Tip** The same year Griffith died, Frank Lloyd Wright's groundbreaking Hollyhock House began construction in Barnsdall Art Park (4800 Hollywood Boulevard, Los Angeles, CA 90027).

45 _ Hare Krishna Cultural Center

A feast for the soul

As you walk down Watseka Avenue on a Sunday evening, the delicious scent of Indian food drifts on the breeze. Nearing the Hare Krishna Cultural Center, you'll come upon a line of perhaps 100 people snaking out the door of its dining room across the street. They are patiently waiting their turn for *prasadam*. Literally translated, *prasadam* means "mercy." In this case, the mercy being offered up is a free weekly dinner. The meal typically consists of spiced rice, a lentil dal, a deep-fried veggie, a cooked veggie like eggplant and tomatoes, paneer, naan, fruit lassi, and some kind of dessert. It's delectable. Everyone is welcome; one does not need to be a member. There is zero proselytizing.

With fluorescent lights and exposed air-conditioning ducts, the dining room is inauspicious. No matter. People of all ages, ethnicities, and economic backgrounds graciously receive what's perceived as "a blessing." The mood is inviting and upbeat. Many of the diners attend the Sunday chantings at the temple just across the street; others simply come for the tradition and / or the lovely feast.

Regardless of what attracts you to *prasadam*, it's a unique opportunity to mix with people you may not meet anywhere else. One family drives for almost three hours, about once a month, to visit. The father, a doctor, has been coming for many years, drawn to the loving atmosphere. Also in attendance are devotees wearing the traditional robes of the Hare Krishna, each with a mark, or *tilaka*, on their forehead. Local residents join the Sunday dinners as well. A young man who grew up in the area, and used to think the temple members were weird, now comes for the friendly vibe and sheepishly admits to enjoying the tasty free food.

So go ahead and strike up a conversation with the person behind you in line or next to you at the table – you never know where a simple "hello" will lead....

Address 3747 Watseka Avenue, Los Angeles, CA 90034, Tel +1 310.836.2676, www.lalive.us | Parking Unmetered street parking | Hours *Prasadam*: Sun 6pm–8pm | Tip Within walking distance is India Sweets and Spices (9409 Venice Boulevard, Los Angeles, CA 90039), an Indian grocery store offering vegetarian and vegan snacks.

46__Harvey House
The last stop for a groundbreaking designer

Mary Elizabeth Jane Colter scared people. Brusque, demanding, and with an incredibly clear vision of what she wanted, she was also a rarity, a trained female architect and designer in the late 19th century, a time when women worked behind the scenes of industry, if at all.

Colter was about 40 years old when the Fred Harvey Company hired her full-time in 1910. Fed up with disgusting train food, Fred Harvey created America's first chain of restaurants, called Harvey House, where fresh comfort food was sold at railroad stations and aboard trains from coast to coast.

The last Harvey House built is in Los Angeles at the stunning Union Station, with a capacious and ravishing interior designed by Colter. Opened in 1939, it's a manifestation of her 38 years as Harvey's chief architect and decorator. Colter had her hand in every detail of the eatery: the Art Deco-style fixtures that masked the train speaker system, the streamline moderne lanterns and lights, the studs on the leather tulle banquet, the delicate bronze-colored circles on the mirrors in the bar evoking champagne bubbles, and the tile floor that mimics the pattern of a Navajo rug. The result is both lighthearted and serious.

Beyond his business ambitions, Harvey had a mission to bring respect to Native-American art and culture in an era when Native Americans were still referred to as savages. Colter was a perfect fit to execute his vision. She created close ties with the Hopi and Navajo tribes, and attended archeological digs, informing her designs. While other big cities were building in the neoclassical style, Colter was committed to vernacular architecture. The 19th-century patrons of Harvey House were thus exposed to the Native-American aesthetic as authentically American, beautiful, and meaningful, and Southwestern style was born – conceived by a private hospitality company with a woman at its helm.

Address Union Station, 800 N Alameda Street, Los Angeles, CA 90012,
www.metro.net/about/art | **Public transport** Any Metro train to Union Station | **Parking**
Paid on-site lot and metered street parking | **Hours** Harvey House is a stop on the free
"Metro Art Moves" Union Station Art & Architecture tour, second Sunday of each month,
10:30am–12:30pm | **Tip** For a deeper dive into Native-American culture, scoot over to
the Autry Museum of the American West (4700 Western Heritage Way, Los Angeles,
CA 90027), which is filled with historical art and artifacts.

47 __Heritage Square Museum
A sanctuary for endangered homes

The Heritage Square Museum is easy to zip by, unnoticed, on the perilous 110 freeway. It consists of eight late-19th-century Victorian structures saved from demolition over the years and moved here from their original locations around Los Angeles. Open to the public, the museum offers guided tours and hosts a number of special themed events throughout the year.

One of the houses particularly stands out due to its unusual octagonal shape. It represents a rare style of Victorian design that didn't catch on. The architect behind the vision was Orson Fowler, considered an eccentric at the time. The house was commissioned by Gilbert Longfellow and built in 1893. He and his wife, Hannah, had raised their several children in an octagonal home built by Fowler on the Atlantic coast. But when Hannah and two of their sons died of tuberculosis, Gilbert moved the family west to Los Angeles in search of cleaner air and more temperate weather. He hired Fowler to build them another octagonal house in Pasadena.

Compared to the ornate and colorful Queen Anne Victorians, Fowler's design is minimalist. The exterior colors are muted with virtually no decorative flourishes. Many interiors of typical Victorian homes are compartmentalized with small rooms that ramble, isolated from one another. Inside the octagon home, the space is open, allowing for a flow of unhindered movement from room to room. Natural light floods in through windows that encircle the house and through the cupola, a small structure on the roof with windows for walls.

Lumber and construction costs were kept down due to each side of the house being of uniform length, requiring shorter spans of wood. Improved air circulation resulting from the many windows reduced heating and cooling costs. Fowler extolled the affordability of this style of home in his book, *The Octagon – A Home for All*, published in 1848.

Address 3800 Homer Street, Los Angeles, CA 90031, Tel +1 323.225.2700, www.heritagesquare.org | **Parking** Unmetered street parking | **Hours** Fri–Sun 11:30am–4:30pm. Guided tours depart hourly, noon–3pm; no self-guided tours allowed. Admission: adults $10, seniors $8, kids (12 & under) $5. | **Tip** Check out the nearby Lummis House (200 E Avenue 43, Los Angeles, CA 90031), a stone craftsman home built during the same era as the Fowler house.

48 Highland Gardens Hotel

Where Joplin spent her final night

Her body sandwiched between the side of the bed and the nightstand, Janis Joplin was found dead of an accidental heroine overdose on October 4, 1970, at what's now the Highland Gardens Hotel. The soulful siren was 27 years old.

Raised middle-class, under the polluted skies of a Texas oil-refinery town called Port Arthur, Joplin felt like a total outsider growing up. Joplin biographer Alice Echols wrote that the rock icon once described Texas as a place that wasn't for people as outrageous as she. It was also segregated, and Janis and her friends often escaped the racist and suffocating culture of their home state by hitting up the music scene in nearby Cajun Louisiana.

Janis's mother, Dorothy East, was probably her first musical influence. Known for her crystal-clear soprano voice, East won a college scholarship but ended up abandoning her dreams of being a singer and snagged a job at the department store Montgomery Ward. Once Janis was old enough, the two often sang together, until East underwent a thyroid operation, which ruined her vocal chords.

Janis went on to sing in church and received praise for her powerful voice. She excelled in school and even skipped second grade. Her self-esteem took a hard hit at 14 when she developed severe acne. Popular no longer, she made a bold choice to seize attention. She cut her school uniform skirt short and doffed the bobby socks in favor of "provocative" tights – just a taste of what was to come.

Joplin had emotions so big, she said to writer Nat Hentoff, "When you feel that much, you have super horrible downs … but … if I hold back, I'm no good *now*, and I'd rather be good sometimes than holding back all the time …"

Sleep in Room 105 where Joplin died. Write on the walls as other visitors do, paying homage to the forever young and complicated musician.

Address 7047 Franklin Avenue, Los Angeles, CA 90028, Tel +1 323.850.0536,
www.highlandgardenshotel.com | **Public transport** Red Line to Hollywood/Highland
Station, then a .5-mile walk | **Parking** Free on-site parking | **Tip** Stop by Barney's Beanery
(8447 Santa Monica Boulevard, West Hollywood, CA 90069), where Joplin and some of
her band members went the night before she died.

49___Highland Park Bowl

Booze and a bowl, no prescription required

When Highland Park Bowl opened its doors in 1927, Prohibition was in full swing. But much like today's marijuana laws, back then a person could receive a prescription that allowed imbibing as a treatment for various ailments. Highland Park Bowl conveniently leased office space to doctors on the second floor who were known for prescribing medicinal whiskey. Patients would march downstairs, doctor's note in hand, to the pharmacy on the first floor to pick up their "medication." And bowl! Because there's nothing like bowling and booze to help heal back pain and all that afflicts you.

Highland Park Bowl set them up and knocked them down until 1966, when Joseph "T" Teresa took over and attempted to modernize the facility by adding drop ceilings and covering the original 1930s mural on the back wall. He also changed the name to Mr. T's Bowl. Over the years, Mr. T's morphed into a live music venue popular with the punk scene of the late 1990s and aughts, while continuing to serve a local boozy clientele. Mr. T passed away in 2005.

Today, the nearly 90-year-old eight-lane alley has been lovingly restored with a thoughtful remodel that harkens back to its origins. Replacing the original BYOB Prohibition ethos are two horseshoe bars under repurposed pin-setting chandeliers and an artisan cocktail menu. Old team name plaques like "The Slow Starters" and other Highland Park Bowl memorabilia line the shelves and walls. Original wooden seating was moved from the lanes to the bar mezzanine and the settee area has been appointed with comfortable leather club sofas.

The former pharmacy area and the front room facing Figueroa Street function as a restaurant serving up rustic pizzas and, in a nod to Mr. T's heyday, a live music venue. All ages are welcome to bowl until 8pm. After that, Highland Park Bowl is open to 21 and older only. Raise a glass. Have a bowl.

Address 5621 N Figueroa Street, Los Angeles, CA 90042, Tel +1 323.257.BOWL, www.highlandparkbowl.com, highlandparkbowl@1933group.com | **Public transport** Gold Line to Highland Park Station, then a .2-mile walk | **Parking** Paid lots and metered street parking | **Hours** Mon–Fri 5pm–2am, Sat & Sun 10am–2am. Prices vary by day and time; check website for details. | **Tip** Civil Coffee (5629 N Figueroa Street, Los Angeles, CA 90042) makes a fine cup of joe and offers delectable small plates like avocado toasts with shitake mushroom "bacon."

50___Holyland Exhibition

Treasures of the real Indiana Jones?

"I'm penniless," declares Betty Shephard, the 88-year old caretaker of the Holyland Exhibition, with a shrug and a rebellious glint in her eyes. She and her daughter live in the building where the collection of religious artifacts started by Antonia F. Futterer, an Australian-born explorer, is kept. Their room and board is paid in exchange for looking after the property and all its treasures, a responsibility Betty takes great pride in.

In 1895, the 24-year-old Futterer left his family to dig for gold in the Australian outback. But he was plagued with bouts of appendicitis and was eventually sent home. As he lay dying, he picked up a Bible and it fell open to Proverbs 3:1, 2: "… let your heart keep my commandments. For length of days and years of life and peace they will add to you." Fervently promising to follow the word of God, Futterer saw his illness vanish.

He later moved to the States, ultimately settling in Los Angeles, and in 1924, he built his home, where he held Bible-study meetings open to all denominations. In 1926, he set off for the Holy Land to search for the Arc of the Covenant. In what's now Jordon, he was lowered into a cave on Mount Nebo and claimed to see a wall of pictures and a tomb sealed with stones; he believed this to be the tomb of Moses, with the Arc in certain proximity, but the Ottomans would not let him dig. It's said Futterer is the inspiration for the fictional film character Indiana Jones.

When you tour the exhibition, mother or daughter, dressed in the attire of a Bedouin, will lead you through four rooms of objects, including primitive oil lamps and jewelry, an ancient eyeliner vial, and tapestries, from Egypt, Damascus, Syria, and other biblical lands. Betty will school you on Bible history with a pointer, authoritatively tapping the genealogical chart, "Futterer's Eye-O-graphic Bible System," showing all the men born of Adam.

Address 2215 Lake View Avenue, Los Angeles, CA 90039, Tel +1 323.664.3162 | **Parking** Unmetered street parking | **Hours** Open daily for tours by appointment only; call ahead. | Grab a bite at Pho Café (2841 Sunset Boulevard, Los Angeles, CA 90026), which offers delicious noodle bowls or soups full of delectable meat or veggies.

51 Homestead Museum
The saga of an old LA family

William Workman shot himself in the head at age 76. No note was left. It was 1876. Once wealthy, he died penniless. The *Los Angeles Herald* reported he was "driven to desperation" knowing that he was left "without means" and that his home would be "swallowed in the vortex."

Originally from England, Workman settled on the eastern edge of Los Angeles and began to successfully raise cattle for tallow and leather. He and his wife built a simple three-room adobe. In the late 1860s, it was remodeled to look like a country home. The renovation literally ensconced the thick adobe walls with new construction.

The combination of flood, drought, and the end of the Gold Rush hit the region hard economically. Reinventing himself, Workman went into dry agriculture, planting crops that required little water; his farm thrived. But his investment in the bank of his son-in-law, F. P. F. Temple, led to his ruin. The financial Panic of 1873 struck and the bank ran out of cash. Facing crippling debt, the family turned to "Lucky" Baldwin, a Wild West business tycoon, and struck an ominous deal, wagering their land for a loan. Temple blew through the borrowed money in two weeks, leaving Workman destitute and suicidal.

Some 30 years later, one of Temple's grandsons accidentally discovered oil on his parents' land. Rich again, the Temple family bought back Workman's original homestead and built La Casa Nueva right next door. Today, you can explore both fully restored buildings, which are open to the public and provide a unique portal into the past. Of particular interest in La Casa Nueva is the homage paid to native and Mexican culture through detailed and colorful painted glass, created at a time when people of Mexican descent were forced to leave the United States in numbers ranging from 500,000 to two million, despite the fact that many were US citizens.

Address 15415 E Don Julian Road, City of Industry, CA 91745, Tel +1 626.968.8492,
www.homesteadmuseum.org, info@homesteadmuseum.org | Parking Free on-site lot | Hours
Tours: Wed–Sun 1pm & 3pm (Workman House), Wed–Sun 2pm & 4pm (La Casa Nueva).
There are no self-guided tours. Admission is free. | Tip Visit the Buddhist Hsi Lai Temple
(3456 Glenmark Drive, Hacienda Heights, CA 91745), where you can enjoy a free tour and
a vegetarian buffet lunch.

52 Idle Hour

A barrel of fun

Los Angeles's population began exploding in the 1840s, growing from 2,000 to 16,000 by the 1870s. Unleashed in the middle of that boom was the Mexican-American War, which concluded in 1848 with the signing of the Treaty of Guadalupe Hidalgo, in Mexico City. The United States was ceded much of Mexico's northern territory, including California. By 1850, California had gained acceptance into the union, officially acquiring statehood.

Giant marketing campaigns, beckoning people to come west for opportunity, worked. Culturally, the nascent metropolis convulsed as it morphed from being a violent and lawless town to at least having some modicum of order. Then, in the 1920s, automobiles were introduced to the streets of LA, and the public got hooked on motoring. The city sprawled. To attract the attention of suburban drivers, businesses invested in thematic architecture – buildings that appeared to be the very thing the business was selling. A few whimsical examples are the Donut Hole in La Puente and the Tamale in Los Angeles.

Idle Hour Cafè was built in 1941 in the shape of a whiskey barrel. It was used as a taproom through the 1960s, became a Flamenco dinner theater, and then fell into disrepair in the 1980s. Under threat of demolition, it was saved by the fervent efforts of *LA* magazine columnist Chris Nichols and designated a Historic-Cultural Monument. Recently purchased and restored by Bobby Green to its original splendor, it's a welcoming place to grab a cocktail and a bite of American comfort food. Old-timey photos capturing the construction of the building line the walls, and the former ceiling planks now serve as flooring.

On the back patio, relocated from Washington Boulevard, is the original Bulldog Café, another example of thematic architecture. Angelenos can still admire the pipe-smoking pooch and even rent him out for small parties.

Address 4824 Vineland Avenue, Los Angeles, CA 91601, Tel +1 818.980.5604, www.idlehourbar.com, becca@1933group.com | **Parking** Metered and unmetered street parking | **Hours** Tue–Sun 11am–2am, Mon 5pm–2am | **Tip** Leave your car and walk five minutes to see a play at the award-winning Crown City Theatre (11031 Camarillo Street, North Hollywood, CA 91602). An intimate space, Crown City is known for staging excellent musicals with quality talent.

53 Inspiration Point at Will Rogers State Park

A ranch to riches story

Raised on a ranch in Oklahoma and born to assimilated and affluent Cherokee parents, Will Rogers grew up in a diverse community made up of African Americans, whites, and Native Americans. He learned how to rope Texas longhorn cattle from a freed slave. His agility with a lasso took him on the road, where he performed in Wild West shows, vaudeville, and the Ziegfield Follies. Hollywood lapped him up, turning him into a giant global star. While he blew audiences away with his lariat tricks, he also laced his shows with folksy, humble but incisive humor. His down-home jokes were adored by audiences and led him to write an incredibly popular weekly column. He satirized politics and had a real love of the everyday American. By the time of his death in 1935, he was such a well-liked guy, it's said as many people came to his funeral ceremony as that of the beloved president Abraham Lincoln.

Rogers, his wife, and children left their Beverly Hills home and settled in the ranch he built in Pacific Palisades. It was there where he roamed the Santa Monica mountains, and what is now the trail leading to Inspiration Point.

While hiking the Inspiration Loop Trail, take a deep breath of fresh Santa Monica air, laden with the scent of chaparral, sage, and maybe a whiff of briny ocean. The wide dirt trail is a moderate two-mile trek. Fragrant eucalyptus trees line a switchback path on the east side. Keep an eye out for birds, like the spotted towhee, the western scrub jay, and Anna's hummingbird. As you ascend to the point, you'll be treated to views of the Santa Monica Mountains and Pacific Ocean in the distance. Once you arrive at the top, you can glory in a 360-degree panorama of Los Angeles, with the giant crescent of the Santa Monica Bay to the west and the jagged profile of Downtown to the east.

Address Will Rogers State Historic Park, 1501 Will Rogers State Park Road, Los Angeles, CA 90272, Tel +1 310.454.8212, www.parks.ca.gov/?page_id=626 | **Parking** Paid on-site lot, $12; senior parking, $11 | **Hours** Daily, including holidays. Parking lot: 8am–sunset. | **Tip** Don't miss the anecdote-filled tour of Will Rogers's rustic ranch house, located in the park. The well-preserved home is decorated with the beloved performer's art and furniture, just as it was when Rogers and his family lived there. Free tours are offered hourly (Thu & Fri 11am–3pm, Sat & Sun 10am–4pm).

54 Institute for Art and Olfaction

Making scents

As you pass through the front door of the Institute for Art and Olfaction on a Wednesday night, the molecules of hundreds of scents, making up a complex blend of florals, bounce through the air and enter the nose. A diverse group of people sits around two long tables, with strips of paper set before them. Their hands are busy. Their faces are bright. Everyone seems happy and engaged. Big smiles welcome newcomers and it's relaxing – the complete antithesis of the high-stakes atmosphere of the corporate perfume industry. Perfumers, also known as noses, concoct the aromatic compounds used in everything from classic colognes to laundry detergents.

Artist Saskia Wilson-Brown opened the Institute for Art and Olfaction as a lab for the scent curious and as an open-source, DIY laboratory. The fragrance world tends to be a closed club with a labyrinthine structure to protect the trade secrets of the perfume-producing mega-companies. An education in the art and science of perfumery is expensive, elitist, and guarded. Not so at the Institute for Art and Olfaction. Weekly sessions are open to all, from novices to experienced blenders, for a nominal fee. Attendees are welcome to draw from the scent organ – a repository of more than 400 scents contained in vials neatly placed on shelves – and carefully craft fragrances while learning the art and chemistry of blending. For those interested in a more structured education, intensive courses as well as beginner classes are also available.

The Institute for Art and Olfaction collaborates regularly with other Los Angeles creative institutions, such as the Hammer Museum and the Getty. It also holds a highly competitive annual award event honoring five independent artisan and experimental perfumers out of a pool of hundreds from more than 20 countries.

Address 932 Chung King Road, Los Angeles, CA 90012, Tel +1 213.616.1744, www.artandolfaction.com, hello@artandolfaction.com | Public transport Gold Line to Chinatown Station, then a .3-mile walk | Parking Paid lots and metered street parking | Hours Wed 3pm–8:30pm (open session starts at 5:30pm, by reservation only); Mon, Tue, Thu, Fri by appointment; closed Sat & Sun | Tip Visit Tin Bo Co (841 N Broadway, Los Angeles, CA 90012), a traditional Chinese herbal medicine store just a short walk away. Herbs and teas are beautifully stored and displayed in glass jars on shelves lining the walls.

55 __It's a Wrap!

As seen on TV

When shows and films would wrap in the 1980s, what the cast and crew didn't claim for themselves in a small auction of wardrobe and props was often thrown away (the environment be darned!). In 1981, Janet Dion saw an opportunity to turn trash into treasure and co-founded a resale shop where production castoffs could potentially find new life and make money too.

It's a Wrap is not a willy-nilly thrift store with dusty instructional dance videos stacked up next to dirty stuffed animals missing eyeballs. It sells the actual clothing and props from completed productions, often from the nearby studios. We're talking Manolo Blahniks, silk Italian suits, Kate Spade dresses, curated vintage garments from period pieces (like an impeccable twin sweater set from the *Astronaut Wives Club*), medical scrubs – okay, so it's not all glamorous. On the walls, iconic film outfits are framed behind glass, such as John Travolta's *Staying Alive* suit. Clothes hang neatly on racks throughout the store, frequently sorted by television or movie title.

Most of the merchandise is sold on consignment, so you can see what production the leopard-print leotard that's captured your fancy came from by how it is tagged. It's a Wrap constantly acquires new inventory, which is housed in a consolidated warehouse, then distributed between two stores, one in Burbank and the other in West Los Angeles.

Don't expect Salvation Army-type bargains. The shop specializes in premium, often name-brand items with very little wear. It's cheaper than buying new, but nothing like the prices you might find across the street from the Burbank location at the American Way Thrift Store. Then again, most secondhand apparel boutiques are not curated by some of the best stylists in Hollywood. You never know what you might unearth at It's a Wrap. And that's the appeal. The thrill of the find is the best part of thrifting.

Address 3315 W Magnolia Boulevard, Burbank, CA 91505, Tel +1 818.567.7366 and
1164 South Robertson Boulevard, Los Angeles, CA 90035, www.itsawraphollywood.com,
movieclothes@aol.com | **Parking** Metered street parking | **Hours** Mon–Fri 11am–7pm,
Sat 11am–6pm, Sun noon–6pm | **Tip** Monte Carlo Deli Pinocchio Restaurant
(3103 W Magnolia Boulevard, Burbank, CA 91505), just two short blocks east, offers
old-school Italian fare (picture roped cheeses hanging from the ceiling).

56 Judson Studios

A light shines through it

Walk into any church with stained glass in Los Angeles and chances are it is the work of the six-generation family legacy of Judson Studios. Located in a quiet corner of Highland Park known as Garvanza, Judson Studios has been meticulously crafting sacred and secular stained glass for more than a century. Examples of their work range from the rotunda skylight at the Natural History Museum to windows in Frank Lloyd Wright's Hollyhock and Ennis houses, with countless places of worship in between.

Founder William Lees Judson never intended to be a purveyor of stained glass. He was a respected painter and teacher, a childhood emigrant from England who ended up in the Arroyo Seco region in search of better health in 1893. He became part of the burgeoning Arts and Crafts movement, painting plein air landscapes that captured the deep greens of California live oaks on rolling hills in soft buttery hues.

William Lees saw a need and desire for stained glass and convinced his three sons who practiced the craft to join him in LA and open a studio. They set up shop in Downtown Los Angeles and quickly established a reputation for quality work.

William Lees kept painting and took a professorship at USC's Los Angeles College of Fine Arts. The campus was built across the street from Lees' home in Garvanza. When the campus burned down nine years later, he escaped through a window and reportedly taught his classes under a pepper tree that day. In 1920, USC would consolidate the art campus with the West Adams campus and Judson Studios would move into the rebuilt Avenue 66 building, where it still operates today. Day to day operations are now in the hands of David Judson, William Lees's great-great-grandson.

Tours go through the former classrooms and studios of USC's fine arts school, now filled with gigantic backlit tables holding stained-glass projects in progress.

Address 200 S Avenue 66, Los Angeles, CA 90042, Tel +1 323.255.0131, www.judsonstudios.com, info@judsonstudios.com | **Parking** Free small on-site lot and unmetered street parking | **Hours** By appointment only. Tours offered to groups of 20 or more. Smaller groups sign up on a waitlist to partner with others to reach the quota. Admission: $10 per person, $8 for students & seniors. | **Tip** While you're in the neighborhood, Stash on York (6000 York Boulevard, Los Angeles, CA 90042, Tel +1 323.999.7474) is a must-visit. The curated vintage and bespoke clothing store is owned by the seamstress Kiki Stash, and is open by appointment only.

57___Kayaking on the Los Angeles River

Big-city rapids

Deluged with relentless rain and wind for five days straight in late February of 1938, the Los Angeles basin was flooded with roaring waters, which killed about 100 people and destroyed 1,500 homes. The Academy Awards were postponed for a week because movie stars were marooned in their houses. The destructive power of the river was recognized. So began the shackling of the wild and wandering ribbon of water that ran through the middle of the city.

The result: much of the LA River became channelized with a concrete bottom. The US Army Corps of Engineers started concreting over the river in the late 1930s; but now, that same entity has approved over a billion dollars to restore it. Through the Corps' recent renewal efforts, the river has reclaimed a semblance of its former glory, especially in Elysian Valley, colloquially known as Frogtown.

One of the most exhilarating ways to experience the river is by kayak. There are various outfits that offer guided tours, and one of the best is LA River Kayak Safari. They combine a bicycle ride upriver with a kayak trip back down.

Riding the river feels practically rebellious. Catching speed from a Class II rapid on an earthen-bottomed waterway restored in the face of massive obstacles in the middle of a dense, intensely urban, sprawling city? Preposterous. Wondrous! Suddenly, you are paddling along 2.5 miles of fresh flowing water, surrounded by coyotes, white and arroyo willows, sycamores, and reeds. On quieter stretches you might hear birds like snowy and great egrets, cormorants, and yellow warblers. Beware, fish! Triumphantly, in the past couple of years, ospreys, rarely seen in urban environments, have started to appear. They have a special claw, like an opposable thumb, that hooks fish out of the water. There are turtles now too. Healing can happen.

Address LA River Kayak Safari, www.lariverkayaksafari.org | Hours The river is open to kayakers four months of the year, from Memorial Day through September. Check LA River Kayak Safari's website for tour schedule. | Tip Walk or bike to Spoke Bicycle Cafe (3050 N Coolidge, Los Angeles, CA 90039), located on the river path, where you can grab a cup of coffee or a snack.

58 L.A. Derby Dolls

Classic banked roller derby with a modern twist

It started in 2003, when Demolicious and Thora Zeen, known off the track as Rebecca Ninburg and Wendy Templeton, recruited skaters via Craigslist with the dream of starting a roller derby league in Los Angeles. The city proved ripe for the sport. From those humble beginnings grew five teams comprising more than 150 skaters and volunteers. Enter the Dolloseum, the self-named Derby Doll coliseum, on a game night and you will typically find the VIP bleachers and general admission floor (standing room only) packed with zealous fans, some toting handmade signs or donning an eagle head, rooting for their favorite team or player. The match is not all camp. Sure, there are a lot of hot pants and fishnets, but these dolls are wicked fierce and true athletes competing for the championship.

But the L.A. Derby Dolls go beyond derby. They are a true community organization with a strong philanthropic bent. Mayor Eric Garcetti rightfully deemed them "a treasure of Los Angeles." Each year, they host Twentywonder, benefiting the Down Syndrome Association of Los Angeles, and have opened their stadium and parking lot for health and job fairs as well as self-defense classes.

The charity tables turned on the Dolls in 2014, when their arena in Filipinotown, west of Downtown, was slated for demolition to make way for condos. The Dolls appealed to their fan base and launched an Indiegogo campaign to raise $100,000 to find and renovate a new location. Within 28 days, they had surpassed their goal. Derby Dolls dismantled their handmade track and relocated it to their new digs in El Sereno near Cal State Los Angeles.

Can't stand to be on the sideline? Strap some skates on those wobbly feet and take a lesson; L.A. Derby Dolls offer training programs on flat or banked tracks, including co-ed scrimmages, a Junior Derby Doll program, and the opportunity to become a Derby Doll yourself.

Address Dolloseum, 4900 Alhambra Avenue, Los Angeles, CA 90032, www.derbydolls.com, questions@derbydolls.com | **Parking** Paid lot and unmetered street parking | **Hours** Season schedule varies; check www.derbydolls.com for details. | **Tip** Nearby is Los Angeles County High School for the Arts (Building #20, 5151 State University Drive, Los Angeles, CA 90032), on the Cal State Los Angeles campus, a prestigious public performing-arts school. Traverse the same grounds walked by notable alumni including Josh Groban and the sisters Haim. The cafe on-site serves food and drinks.

59 Leo Politi Mural
Painting over the past

In 1931, at the age of 22, artist Leo Politi left Italy and came to Los Angeles by way of the Panama Canal. He was deeply influenced by the rural cultures of South and Central America, which informed his artwork throughout his lifetime. Politi settled in LA's Bunker Hill. He became a figure on nearby Olvera Street, where he frequently sketched and painted, selling his work amid the other vendors. Decades later, he would paint his well-known mural *The Blessing of the Animals*, which still stands today in Olvera Street's Paseo de la Plaza.

Politi made a name for himself in children's literature. His illustrations capture Olvera Street, Bunker Hill, and Angelino Heights long before a freeway cut through Downtown and the neighborhood's charming Victorian homes were razed to make way for the high-rises of today. In 1950, he won the prestigious Caldecott Medal for *Song of the Swallows*, his illustrated children's book about the long annual journey of the swallow from Mexico to San Juan Capistrano.

Less well known is Politi's mural at the South Pasadena Public Library. Politi originally painted the scene on a series of panels inside the children's section of the library in 1957 for $200. In 1982, after the library underwent extensive remodeling, Politi returned to freshen up the mural, offering his service free of charge. But instead of restoring the painting, Politi completely reworked it, controversially creating a brighter palette and slightly altering the scene. He replaced the cat with a dog, and painted over the original ochre hues (which were reflective of his early works, such as *Pedro, the Angel of Olvera Street*) with the vibrant blues and greens he favored later in his career.

In tribute to the legacy of Politi, who passed away in 1996, the library unveiled a newly cast bronze Politi sculpture, which can be seen at the Oxley Street entrance.

Address South Pasadena Public Library, 1100 Oxley Street, South Pasadena, CA 91030, Tel +1 626.403.7340 | Public transport Gold Line to South Pasadena/Mission Station, then a .2-mile walk | Parking Unmetered street parking | Hours Mon–Wed 11am–9pm, Thu–Fri 11am–6pm, Sat 10am–5pm, Sun 1pm–5pm | Tip The ever-changing window displays at Koi (1007 Fair Oaks Avenue, South Pasadena, CA 91030) never disappoint. The women's clothing and accessories inside are equally fabulous.

60__Libros Schmibros

A book and a cozy nook

Unlike any other lending library, Libros Schmibros, located in East LA's Mariachi Plaza, isn't too concerned about the borrowed books being returned to the stacks. The man behind the institution, David Kipen, only cares that more people are reading. In fact, prior to returning to Los Angeles, he headed the National Reading Initiatives by the National Endowment for the Arts and launched the Big Read and the One Book One City campaigns. With Libros Schmibros, Kipen's mission remains the same: open and improve lives through literature.

A visit to the library, with its floor-to-ceiling bookshelves and big wooden tables usually full of local Schmibrodites, is like getting reading therapy. Tell Kipen what you like and he'll curate a collection of titles sure to suit your taste. If you have the means, give a little love and become a donor member. You'll go home with a T-shirt or tote bag, just like public radio, and an armful of books.

But Libros Schmibros isn't just about the cool schwag. It's about literacy, community service with plenty of volunteer opportunities, and a bit of artistic happening as well. Curated donations are accepted but must be vetted prior to drop-off. Details are on their website. Among the many events and outreach, the library hosts workshops for eastside writers by eastside writers. Kipen also ventures west to host a book club at the Hammer Museum in Westwood. And in true mobile outreach mode, Libros Schmibros has a fleet of "bicycle libraries." Each two-wheeled bookmobile is outfitted to carry forty books each, date-stamped with a card, old-school lending-library style. Volunteer cyclists choose their own selection of books and bike the neighborhood in search of readers. With any luck, the recipients will wend their way to Libros Schmibros, tome in hand, ready to exchange and venture deeper into the expansive world of literature.

Address 1711 Mariachi Plaza de Los Angeles, Los Angeles, CA 90033,
Tel +1 323.688.4850, www.librosschimbros.org | Public transport Gold Line to
Mariachi Plaza Station | Parking Metered and unmetered street parking | Hours Thu–Sun
noon–6pm | Tip Solicit a mariachi band for a quinceañera or backyard party at Mariachi
Plaza. Many bands charge by the number of musicians and hours played. Please note, all-
female mariachi bands are rare and typically cost more than all-male or mixed groups. Olé!

61 Los Angeles Science Fantasy Society

Where Ray Bradbury got his start

A group of Los Angeles Science Fantasy Society (LASFS) members meets every Thursday night, sitting on foldout chairs, in a fluorescent-lit room, going over minutes, "or menace" as they are jokingly called. Friday nights are more playful, since they're generally devoted to gaming of all kinds, including fantasy role-play, board games, and cards. Second Sundays of the month are the most leisurely gatherings. Members and visitors might bring meals, since they can hang out all day. It's an opportunity to meld with like-minded sci-fi and fantasy fans.

Such bonding has been going on since 1934, when LASFS, the longest continuously running sci-fi and fantasy club in the world, started holding meetings. Back then, members, including Ray Bradbury, would assemble regularly at Clifton's Cafeteria (see p. 52) in Downtown LA, where they would scoop out the free limeade that gushed through the first-floor fountain.

There are a few different spaces where members can hang out on broken-in couches to chat or watch movies. The room where video game nights are held houses about five computers. The library – brightly lit with neatly organized volumes – demonstrates an obvious reverence for the society's passion. More than 25,000 sci-fi and fantasy books fill the shelves for members to borrow and enjoy. (Guests may read books in the library, but can't check them out.)

All types of sci-fi buffs are members. You might run into the unassuming author John de Chancie, or Hugo-award winners Larry Niven and Jerry Pournelle. There are also non-authors such as Michael Galloway. Self-described as mischievous, with a white beard and spectacles askew, he taught Dungeons & Dragons for 34 years. Some regulars, like Marty Cantor, publisher of the LASFS's newsletter, have been enjoying the camaraderie and fellowship of the society for decades.

Address 6012 Tyrone Avenue, Van Nuys, CA 91401, Tel +1 818.904.9544, www.lasfsinc.info, webmaster@lasfsinc.info | **Parking** Unmetered street parking | **Hours** Meetings: Thu & Fri 8pm. Open houses are held on the second Sunday of the month, usually at 2pm. Nonmembers are welcome, but call in advance to schedule a time to visit. | **Tip** Stay "cool" at the old-school and slightly run-down Iceland Ice Skating Center (14318 Calvert Street, Van Nuys, CA 91401), where they actually have bumper-car sessions.

62 Machine Project
The art of making

Something interesting is always happening at the Echo Park arts collective, founded by Mark Allen. Lots of arts organizations talk about blurring the line between audience and artist, but Machine Project really does it. Exhibits in the gallery space on Alvarado Street are linked to themed events and hands-on workshops. Take artist Josh Beckman's *Sea Nymph*. A realistic replica of a masted wooden ship was constructed to look as if it was half sunk in the gallery floor. Throughout the seven-week exhibit, Machine Project brought in different artists and experts to host nautical-themed events around the shipwreck: a lecture on how not to get lost at sea, a knot-tying workshop, a *Moby Dick* puppet show, a jellyfish crochet class, and many more.

Machine Project also offers rotating classes that have included welding, sewing and patternmaking, and special-effects makeup (including techniques for creating blisters, boils, and open wounds at Halloween time). Workshops are open to all; members receive discounts.

Machine Project moves beyond its gallery too. The collective famously took over LACMA in 2008 and invigorated exhibits and halls by incorporating performance art and humor. Strolling minstrels in the Art of Americas building serenaded visitors enjoying chair massages. Opera singers belted out live elevator music; drum soloists with an entire kit provided percussion in the elevator bank next door. Kinetic sculptures walked the courtyard. Machine Project did something similar in 2014, with the Pasadena Gamble House. Poetry readings were held in closets, nighttime tours were led by flashlight, and workshops reflected the Arts and Crafts tradition endemic of the Gamble House, such as an Art Nouveau embroidery tutorial, a natural plant preservation and perfumery class, and a séance to boot. The best part is that these experiences don't happen without the audience participating as co-artist.

Address 1200 N Alvarado, Los Angeles, CA 90026, Tel +1 213.483.8761, www.machineproject.com, machine@machineproject.com | Parking Metered street parking | Hours Unofficially open most days 11am–6pm & usually an hour before evening events; check website for schedule. | Tip Burrito King at Sunset and Alvarado (2109 Sunset Boulevard, Los Angeles, CA 90026) was lionized in the Tom Waits song "Emotional Weather Report" as the classy joint where he takes himself out on a date. Cheap eats.

63 Moore Lab of Zoology

Birds of a feather flocked together

Following in the footsteps of John James Audubon, ornithologist Robert Moore studied birds the old-fashioned way, by shooting them with a rifle, examining the carcasses, and stuffing them. Moore amassed a collection of more than 50,000 birds. Truth be told, Moore had help, primarily from Chester Lamb, who contributed 44,000 specimens and was paid around $1 to $2 a pop – an extraordinary accomplishment, especially considering Lamb had a glass eye. The specimens, some dating back over 100 years, contain invaluable genetic information that informs bird ecology and conservation today. Moore's beautiful assemblage, including more than 6,500 hummingbirds, can still be viewed by appointment at Occidental College's Moore Lab of Zoology (MLZ).

The MLZ is a working laboratory located behind the campus's biosciences building. A giant topographical map of Mexico, a vibrant area for bird diversity in the late 1800s and the primary origin of Moore's specimens, hangs in the mid-bank stairway leading up to the lab. At the top of the stairwell are offices featuring a beautiful display of taxidermied scrub jays. Entering into the lab itself, you may find students engaged in prepping skins or studying DNA extracted from specimens. A door at the far end opens to rows of metal boxes neatly stacked one on top of another with the front lids held by sash locks. When the lids are pulled away, wooden trays reveal specimens with tags in neat Victorian script documenting each one's Latin name, sex, date and location of collection, and who procured it.

The riotously colorful tray of hummingbirds dazzles the eye with luminescent gorgets of red, blue, and green. A swordbill humming-bird (*Ensifera ensifera*), the only bird with a beak longer than its body, occupies the same tray as the smallest bird species, the bumblebee hummingbird (*Calypte helenae*), truly not much larger than its namesake.

Address Occidental College, 1600 Campus Road, Los Angeles, CA 90041,
Tel +1 323.259.1320, www.oxy.edu/moore-lab-zoology, mlzbirds@gmail.com | Parking
Obtain a free parking permit from Campus Safety. Park in green or unmarked spaces only.
Off-campus unmetered street parking also available. | Hours By appointment only; call or
email to schedule in advance. | Tip Pat and Lorraine's Coffee Shop (4720 N Eagle Rock
Boulevard, Los Angeles, CA 90041) is a simple Mexican-influenced diner, which happens
to be the cafe setting where a fictional group of thieves in Quentin Tarantino's premier film
Reservoir Dogs meet to plan their heist.

64 Mosaic Tile House

A million little pieces

Over a period of almost two decades the husband-and-wife artist team of Cheri Pann and Gonzolo Duran have transformed their formerly nondescript stucco home in Venice into a vibrant Antonio Gaudi-like ever-evolving mosaic masterpiece.

Pann and Duran met and fell in love later in life. And the evidence of their romance radiates throughout their work and living spaces. It even spills out of a ceramic fortune cookie in the front yard in the form of mosaicked promises of affection.

When the couple bought their house in 1994, the priority was to add on a studio in back. Pann, then in her fifties, took classes at Santa Monica City College to learn construction. While building the studio, the duo began to retile the bathroom. When some of the tiles broke, the artists embraced the jagged pieces and embarked on their mosaic adventure. Behind the sink near the floor, a small section of four-inch-square tiles marks the beginning of what has become a lifelong project. One room quickly led to another and eventually, they covered nearly every square inch of the house. The results are exuberant, playful, and truly astonishing.

Duran and Pann said they had so much fun indoors, they moved on to the outdoor areas and continue to create mosaics from pottery and ceramic donations that are dropped off by friends and fans, as well as from tiles fired in their own kilns.

Visitors, by reservation, can enter their home and witness this stunning expression of their personal and creative collaboration. Despite the bold colors, the whimsical spaces exude a sense of calm vitality, a strong work ethic, and, of course, the artists' love – for each other, for the work itself, and, by extension, for those who come to witness this eccentric celebration of individuality and imagination.

Just try to leave without a smile plastered across your face – go on – we dare you.

Address 1116 Palms Boulevard, Venice, CA, 90291, www.mosaictilehouse.com, mosaictilehouse@mac.com | **Parking** Unmetered street parking | **Hours** By appointment only, Fri & Sat 11am–3pm. Tours are $12 per person. | **Tip** For another take on mosaic house art, check out the Farnam family's bungalow (corner of California Avenue and 26th Street, Santa Monica, CA 90403); the home is covered in tiles, from top to bottom.

65 __ Mount Wilson Observatory
A star-studded event

In its day – we're talking 1908 – the 60-inch telescope atop Mount Wilson was an astonishment. The world's then most powerful telescope was funded by library builder Andrew Carnegie and designed by solar magnetic field discoverer George Ellery Hale. In the hands of scientist Harlow Shapley, the massive scope proved the sun was not the center of the Milky Way. It was the largest telescope in the world until 1917, when the 100-inch Hooker Telescope, also designed by Hale, was built mere steps away.

The Mount Wilson Observatory is an amazing place steeped in history and astronomical discoveries. Albert Einstein and Edwin Hubble's eyeballs peered through the optics at Mount Wilson. What they saw helped them solve the mysteries in their minds and define the unfolding laws of physics and the cosmos.

Long outdated by Hubble technology for scientific discovery, the 60-inch telescope's primary function now is public outreach. Tours, including entry to the telescopes, are available weekends from April to December. Private tours can also be booked year-round. Best of all, the scope can be rented, along with an astronomer to help navigate the night sky and operate the machinery, for a half night or whole night of viewing (for fees of $950 and $1700 respectively). Groups of up to 25 people aged 12 and older can channel their inner Einstein and examine the constellations through the scope. The observatory also offers public viewing nights, when individuals can survey the sky for $110 to $325.

In 2009, a huge forest fire known as the Station Fire, caused by arson, came perilously close to Mount Wilson, charring trees mere feet away from paved trails near the Hooker Telescope. Look carefully and you can still see the burned area and blackened oaks, a reminder of just how dangerously close a national treasure came to being erased forever.

Address Mount Wilson Observatory, Mount Wilson Road, Pasadena, CA 91106, Tel +1 626.304.0269, www.mtwilson.edu, tours@mtwilson.edu (to arrange a private tour), mtwilsontelescopes@gmail.com (to reserve an observation session) | Parking On-site lot. Adventure Pass required. Daily passes available for purchase at the Cosmic Cafe and other adventure retailers. | Hours Daily 10am–5pm, weather permitting. Tours: Apr–Dec, Sat & Sun 1pm & 2pm; $15 general admission. Telescope observation sessions by appointment or on scheduled nights, Apr–Dec; see website for details. | Tip The on-site Cosmic Cafe (open Apr–Nov), offers simple sandwiches and a map for a self-guided tour.

66__Museum of Broken Relationships
Art of the broken heart

Heartbreak is a universal language. Perhaps that is why the exhibits at the Museum of Broken Relationships resonate so strongly. What began as a traveling exhibit in 2006 by two Croatian artists – an ex-couple – morphed into an ever-evolving collection now housed in a permanent location in Croatia's capital Zagreb. Founders Olinka Vištica and Dražen Grubišić reached out to friends and culled together artifacts of severed romance, the objects left behind long after the lovers have gone – letters, fuzzy handcuffs, the actual detritus that takes up space in the backs of countless closets and drawers.

While vacationing in April 2015, Los Angeles power attorney John Quinn stumbled upon the museum and was blown away. He envisioned a sister museum in Los Angeles. Ten months and a licensing deal later, his dream became a reality when the Museum of Broken Relationships opened its doors in the former Frederick's of Hollywood lingerie store.

Step past the bustle and griminess of Hollywood Boulevard and enter the museum's white high-ceilinged modern gallery. A dramatic chandelier of black metal lights hangs over exquisitely crafted display cases filled with relics of ruptured romance. A diamond ring with the caption, "s(he) be(lie)ve(d)." A plaster-of-Paris sculpture of large breasts unnaturally close together, donated by a woman whose ex asked that she wear it when they had sex. The shredded jeans of a husband permanently brain damaged after he crashed into an elk on his motorcycle. The wife's story, typed on cream-colored paper mounted on a metal plaque, says his body survived, they are still married, but the person he once was is now lost forever. Beauty, agony, and humor are all powerfully communicated through these objects, striking a chord with everyone who has ever loved and watched it wither.

Address 6751 Hollywood Boulevard, Los Angeles, CA 90028, Tel +1 323.892.1200,
www.brokenships.la, museum@brokenships.la | **Public transport** Red Line to Hollywood/
Highland Station, then a .1-mile walk | **Parking** Paid lots and metered street parking |
Hours Mon 11am–5pm, Tue & Wed 11am–7pm, Thu & Sun 11am–8pm, Fri & Sat
11am–9pm | **Tip** Sit in a red booth at Musso & Frank Grill (6667 Hollywood Boulevard,
Los Angeles, CA 90028), Hollywood's first restaurant; swill a martini and think of the
glamorous icons of Hollywood, like Clark Gable and Carole Lombard, who spent many
an hour warming the very same seats.

67_Museum of Death
To live and die in LA

The Museum of Death is not for the faint of heart. The macabre collection centers around the more grisly aspects of kicking the bucket, with a heavy emphasis on serial killers.

Richard Ramirez, otherwise known as the Satan-loving Night Stalker, who terrorized California in the mid-1980s, has a display case all to himself featuring a few of his former possessions, a porn magazine, and some of his writing excerpts with thoughts on what makes a good night. Not to spoil the reveal, but it includes a full moon, sex, and drugs. Opposite is a wall full of clown drawings and paintings by murderer, rapist, and pedophile John Wayne Gacy. A small room in the back is dedicated to the Manson family. Charles Manson's 12-string Epiphone guitar is mounted on the wall behind protective glass, while a dirty quilt, hand-stitched by the Manson women, hangs openly to the right, and a documentary including interviews with Charles Manson runs on a loop – a testament to how Los Angeles dreams of fame can go horrifically wrong.

Speaking of cults, the Museum of Death acquired a collection of artifacts from the compound of the Heaven's Gate cult when 38 members and their leader donned Nike sneakers and purple shrouds before ingesting a toxic concoction of phenobarbital-laced applesauce and vodka, in hopes of catching a ride on a space ship trailing the Hale-Bopp comet. The museum was originally established in San Diego, but was denied a lease renewal largely because of its publicized efforts to recreate a diorama of the Heaven's Gate death scene. The collection relocated to Hollywood, bringing the controversial diorama with them.

Oddly beautiful and haunting are the Victorian pictures of child corpses. The custom was to photograph the dead in an open casket, often with flowers artfully arranged in the coffin. The result is a solemn and dignified tribute to the end of a life.

Address 6031 Hollywood Boulevard, Hollywood, CA 90028, Tel +1 323.466.8011, www.museumofdeath.net, museumofdeath@sbcglobal.net | Public transport Red Line to Hollywood/Vine Station, then a .3-mile walk | Parking Free on-site lot | Hours Sun–Thu 11am–8pm, Fri 11am–9pm, Sat 11am–10pm; $15 admission | Tip Capitol Records (1750 Vine Street, Los Angeles, CA 90028), less than a half mile away, is called the House That Nat Built, in recognition of the enormous capital Nat King Cole brought to Capitol.

68_Museum of Jurassic Technology

A cabinet of curiosities

Many people claim to be geniuses. Museum of Jurassic Technology founder and curator David Wilson really is one. In 2001, Wilson was awarded a MacArthur genius grant that helped keep the doors open to the eclectic trove of artifacts and exhibits that make up the Museum of Jurassic Technology.

Visitors typically deeply love or vehemently hate the museum. Very few leave apathetic. The small, dimly lit labyrinth of rooms unfolds like a dusty cabinet of curiosities, housing exhibits like the Garden of Eden on Wheels, an homage to razed Los Angeles trailer parks with dioramas of miniature mobile homes set back into the walls and excavated artifacts under glass in the center of the room. Where did Grandma's collection of ceramic promotional alcohol decanters go? Well, it might be right here.

The exhibit in a back room on vulgar remedies, past a bank of microscopes focused on tiny mosaics crafted from butterfly scales, is a reminder that your mom's suggestion to use spit and tears to disinfect a scrape actually works. After all, the development of penicillin was born from the accidental discovery of the healing properties of moldy bread. Fortunately, the practice of curing childhood bedwetting by administering mice on toast has fallen out of favor.

Upstairs in the bright Tula Tea Room, complimentary cookies and tea are served, and borzoi hounds lounge on padded benches alongside patrons. A flight of stairs off the tearoom leads to a rooftop garden with Moroccan-style arches that doubles as an aviary for "ceremonial" white – and frequently amorous – doves. Originally bred in captivity, the doves are refugees from wedding and event releases rescued from around Los Angeles. If you are lucky, David Wilson himself might be in the aviary, playing an instrument or tending to the nesting hutch.

Address 9341 Venice Boulevard, Culver City, CA 90232, Tel +1.310.836.6131, www.mjt.org, info@mjt.org | **Public transport** Expo Line to Culver City Station, then a .7-mile walk | **Parking** Metered and unmetered street parking | **Hours** Thu 2pm–8pm, Fri & Sat noon–6pm. Admission: $8 general, $5 students & seniors, kids 12 and under free. | **Tip** Surfas Culinary District (8777 West Washington Boulevard, Culver City, CA 90232) is a kitchen supply store that opened in 1937 and puts other shops of the same ilk to shame. Pick up pastry bags and tips, industrial mixers, gourmet cheeses, and more, or stop by the side cafe for a quick bite.

69 Music Box Staircase

What goes up must come down

In the Academy Award-winning short film, *The Music Box*, three times do "businessmen" Laurel and Hardy laboriously push and pull a boxed piano up multiple flights of a steep staircase. Three times does their cargo take a clamorous tumble down the steps while Laurel and Hardy, out of breath and exhausted, look on despondently. Finally, on their fourth and successful attempt, they arrive at the customer's door, where a chipper postman informs them that all they had to do was take their horse-drawn delivery cart up a different street directly to the front door, avoiding the staircase altogether. With this, the geniuses choose to go down that treacherous staircase with the piano again to take the simpler route.

Those 133 well-trodden steps are a public staircase linking the one-way Descanso Drive and Vendome Street. When the film was shot, large swaths of undeveloped land lined the south and north sides of the stairs. Now, when you walk up the eleven flights, all around you are homes nestled into the hills. While the environs have changed, the unremarkable concrete stairs look exactly the same as they did when they were immortalized by the comedy duo.

There are many hidden staircases sprinkled around Los Angeles. In the pre-automobile era, they served to connect pedestrians to trolleys, buses, and trains. They also provided a safer route down the city's steep hills. There's the meandering Beachwood Canyon Staircase, which takes you through old Hollywood. It includes a section – at the corner of North Beachwood and Woodshire Drives – that's a double set of steps separated by planter boxes, which apparently once held a running stream. Also popular are the famous Santa Monica Stairs, loaded with weekend warriors, at 7th Street and Entrada Drive. Though many of these staircases are no longer widely used, they're a charming reminder of an earlier car-free time, before Angelenos started driving to take a walk.

Address The bottom of the staircase is next to 935 Vendome Avenue, Los Angeles, CA 90026; the top is between 3270 and 3778 Descanso Drive, Los Angeles, CA 90026 | Parking Unmetered street parking | Hours Always open | Tip To explore more of Los Angeles's outdoor staircases, check out www.laclimbingthehiddenstairways.blogspot.com.

70 The Musical Road

Hi-yo Silver!

Few come to Lancaster, near the northern border of Los Angeles County, where east/west avenues are named by letter and the north/south streets by number, just to take in the sites – not that Lancaster is without its own idiosyncratic charms. The city is home to Edwards Air Force Base, the site of numerous landings for the now defunct space shuttle program. The Houston Astros host a Single-A minor-league team in Lancaster, the JetHawks, with a Kinetic Brewery beer garden on the third base line. A local rustic church served as the fictional Two Pines Chapel, where the ill-fated wedding rehearsal in Quentin Tarantino's *Kill Bill* was interrupted by a visit from the Deadly Viper Assassination Squad. And each spring, the Antelope Valley Poppy Reserve draws visitors hoping to see the mountains exploding with orange blooms.

If you happen to be en route to the reserve, take the left lane on Avenue G to enjoy what is Lancaster's most eccentric feature: the Musical Road, a brief quarter mile of asphalt that reproduces the melody of the "William Tell Overture" – more commonly known as the Lone Ranger theme song – as cars drive over it.

The "singing" roadway was originally built at a site about four miles from its current location by the Honda Corporation for a commercial filmed in 2008. By cutting grooves in the pavement at different intervals, Honda's team of engineers was able to create timed musical notes as tires rolled over the grooves at 55 miles per hour, the posted speed limit. A mere 18 days later, the road was repaved due to some of the area residents' ardent complaints about the constant noise caused by curious motorists at all hours of the day and night.

Evidently, the naysayers were in the minority. The Musical Road was reinstated by popular demand just three months later – this time on a secluded stretch of roadway, two miles from any private home.

Address 3187 W Avenue G, Lancaster, CA 93536 | Getting there By car: head west on Avenue G just over a mile from the freeway. Follow the signs for the Musical Road. Stay in the far left lane to participate. | Hours Always open | Tip Fans of Quentin Tarantino can visit the Two Pines Chapel (19857 - 19999 E Avenue G, Lancaster, CA 93535), featured in *Kill Bill*, 28 miles east of the Musical Road.

71_Neon Retro Arcade
The greatest hits of coin-op video games

There was a party. There was a pinball machine. There were sparks flying. That's what was going down when Mia Mazadiego and Mark Gunther met and fell for each other in 2002. It seems apropos, therefore, that the couple went on to open a 1980s and 1990s-era arcade, where walking down an aisle feels like stepping back in time – except that it's not so dank inside. Occupying a cheerful space with hanging cafe lights, about 50 classic arcade games and 7 pinball machines beckon to visitors: "Remember me and all those good times we had? I'm still here for you."

Generally speaking, the 20-somethings get fired up when they catch sight of Street Fighter 2, The Simpsons, and Ninja Turtle. The 30- and 40-somethings make a beeline for PacMan, Centipede, and Asteroids. Preteens find their home at Neon too. They've been watching YouTube videos of the classics and come excited to play the real things. What those young'uns don't experience is the use of quarters. The business model of Neon is free play. You pay a per-hour fee ($10) and can start and restart a game at will – no need to place your coins "on deck," claiming your right to go next. There's one rule though – no game hogging, which, according to Mazadiego and Gunther, has, remarkably, never happened. Many of the games are multiplayer and often those playing are glad to let others join in, ramping up the competition and fun.

The whole arcade phenomena really started with the Atari game, Pong, in 1972. The play was elegantly simple. Based on the sport of table tennis, two paddles hit a ball over a net. Whoever gets to eleven points first wins. The story goes, one of the Atari founders plopped down the first Pong game in a bar to see if it held interest. In a week and a half, the console was having mechanical difficulties. It turned out the problem was that too many quarters were blocking the coin mechanism. Popular indeed.

Address 28 S Raymond Avenue, Pasadena, CA 91105, Tel +1 626.568.2924, www.neonretroarcade.com | Parking Paid lots and metered street parking | Hours Mon, Wed & Thu 3pm–10pm, Fri 3pm–midnight, Sat 11am–midnight, Sun 11am–9pm | Tip Head east to the sprawling and diverse Huntington Library, Art Collections, and Botanical Gardens (1151 Oxford Road, San Marino, CA 91108). Highlights include the more than 14 geographic gardens, particularly the Chinese, Japanese, and Desert Gardens.

72 The Nethercutt Collection and Museum

Every car will break your heart

Is it possible to have a giant crush … on a car? The answer is a breathtaking yes, if you visit the Nethercutt. Your heart will race as you lay eyes on the staggering showroom displays, overflowing with hunky and charismatic automobiles from 1904 to 1973, including specimens from Packard, Cord, Duesenberg, Auburn, Pierce-Arrow, and Rolls Royce.

The museum's founder, J. B. Nethercutt (1913–2004), was raised by his aunt, Merle Norman, after his mother passed away. Norman was busy making cosmetics on her cookstove, while her nephew studied chemistry at CalTech. After graduating, Nethercutt joined his aunt's business and together they built up the Merle Norman Cosmetics empire, making millions. Nethercutt's wealth went to accumulating an astounding array of cars.

It is a bit overwhelming, gazing upon these giant works of art with their many fine details: decorative radiators, elegant taillights, finely crafted mascots, and stunning stone guards (see the 1928 Isotta Fraschini – wow!). Most were driven by the rich and powerful, and it shows. Some have chauffeur speakers and a passenger microphone.

Take time to admire the 1930 Packard, intended as a gift for the wife of an executive at Hupp Motor Company. When she died before ever seeing the car, the bereft widower told his chauffeur to junk the beauty. The chauffeur eschewed orders and secreted it away at his home, never driving it. Discovered nearly 40 years later, it was snapped up by Nethercutt and restored.

As your visit winds down and your vehicular romance comes to an end, you may find that initial heart-thumping infatuation has turned to love and respect – respect for the spirit of innovation, confidence, and boldness it took to create these divine bodies of motor.

Address The Nethercutt Collection and Museum, 15151 Bledsoc Street (Museum) and 15200 Bledsoe Street (Collection), Sylmar, CA 91342, Tel +1 818.364.6464, www.ncthercuttcollection.org, info@nethercuttcollection.org | **Parking** Free on-site lot | **Hours** Museum: Tue–Sat 9am–4:30pm. Collection: open only for guided tours by appointment Thu, Fri & Sat 10am or 1:30pm; admission is free. | **Tip** Need to cool down after a few hours of auto lust? Visit the Hansen Dam Aquatic Center (11798 Foothill Boulevard, Lake View Terrace, CA 91342), a sprawling recreational facility with a 1.5-acre swimming pool and 9-acre lake.

73__New Beverly Cinema

Something old, new, borrowed, and blue

Just west of La Brea Boulevard, a 228-seat revival theater has remained in operation since 1978. The building dates back to the late 1920s, starting out as a candy shop and later reinventing itself as a vaudeville venue, a nightclub, the 1936 headquarters of the California Republican Assembly, and finally a pornographic theater.

In 1978, Sherman Torgan bought the place and made an honest movie theater out of it by screening classics. Viewers didn't get comfortable seats, but they got a cheap ticket and affordably priced concessions. When Torgan died, in 2007, the New Beverly went black and was under the threat of redevelopment.

Quasi-comedy-epic-tragedy filmmaker Quentin Tarantino, who had been giving Torgan about $5,000 a month previously to keep the theater open, stepped in and bought it outright. Tarantino is famously quoted in the *Hollywood Reporter* as saying, "As long as I'm alive, and as long as I'm rich, the New Beverly will be there, showing double features in 35mm." Michael Torgan, Sherman's son, managed the theater until 2014, when Tarantino took over scheduling after seven years of ownership.

Classic midnight screenings and children's weekend matinees (including free kids' popcorn) are hallmarks of the New Beverly. Thankfully, the spine spiraling seats were reupholstered in 2014, making the still low cost of admission a bargain that no longer requires a follow-up visit to the chiropractor.

A revival theater is a poor person's cinema master class, in this case, taught vicariously by the self-educated film fanatic Tarantino through his curated screenings. Many of the movies shown are borrowed from his sizeable private collection, which spans genres and time periods, from action-packed Bruce Lee kung fu flicks to classics by Orson Wells. Buy a bag of popcorn, sit down, and pay attention. One of the most influential contemporary filmmakers has something great to share.

Address 7165 Beverly Boulevard, Los Angeles, CA 90036, Tel +1 323.938.4038, www.thenewbev.com, info@thenewbev.com | **Parking** Metered street parking | **Hours** Mon–Sun 6am–10pm | **Tip** République (624 S La Brea Avenue, Los Angeles, CA 90036), about a mile south of the theater on La Brea, may have the best fries in Los Angeles, according to Pulitzer Prize-winning food critic Jonathan Gold. The restaurant is open for lunch and dinner.

74__Norton Simon Museum
Portrait of a lady, by a lady

Norton Simon, the multimillionaire industrialist, had incredible taste. Need proof? Gaze upon his personal art collection housed at the intimate and mighty Norton Simon Museum. Thoughtfully curated paintings and sculptures representing a broad range of artists and eras load the rooms. One example is the portrait of Theresa, Countess Kinsky, by Elisabeth Louise Vigèe Le Brun, best known as the portraitist of Marie Antoinette.

The painting of the 25-year-old countess was made seven years after she was left by her husband of one day, when he returned to his mistress. She wouldn't remarry until she was in her forties. Kinsky received Le Brun's royal treatment. She's richly attired in a deep blue velvet dress, with a diaphanous golden shawl lifted by a gust of wind. Loose curls and a direct gaze suggest a woman self-possessed, much like her portraitist.

Vigèe Le Brun showed early prowess as an artist. Her father taught her to paint, but he died when she was only 12, and she was left without a mentor. Taken under the wing of two artist friends of the family, her casual education continued.

At 22, she was called to the palace to paint Marie Antoinette. She went on to immortalize the ill-fated queen on canvas about 30 times. The king of France requested her admittance into the prestigious Académie Royale de Peinture et de Sculpture, and, at 28, she was one of only four women accepted.

Le Brun painted the portrait of Countess Kinsky while self-exiled in Vienna in 1793, four years into the French Revolution, during the bloody Reign of Terror. That's the year Marie Antoinette, the most loyal supporter of her work, was executed. Fearing persecution herself, Le Brun had fled France with her nine-year-old daughter shortly after the revolution began. She went on to travel the world for 12 years, creating portraits of world luminaries.

Address 411 W Colorado Boulevard, Pasadena, CA 91105, Tel +1 626.449.6840, www.nortonsimon.org | **Parking** Free on-site lot | **Hours** Mon, Wed & Thu noon–5pm, Fri & Sat 11am–8pm, Sun 11am–5pm, closed Tue. Admission: $12 adults, $9 seniors, kids are free. | **Tip** Explore another one of Pasadena's hidden gems, and take a tour of the historic Gamble House (4 Westmoreland Place, Pasadena, CA 91103, www.gamblehouse.org), designed by the expert Craftsman-style architects Greene and Greene.

75___Orcutt Ranch

The oldest citrus orchard in town

While William Warren Orcutt did not discover the dinosaur fossils at what is now the La Brea Tar Pits, he was the first person to identify and legitimize the bones as belonging to the mighty lizards, in 1901. Early settlers and Native Americans were aware of the remains, but assumed they were from cattle and other regional animals. Orcutt, a petroleum geologist, involved the paleontology department at the University of California at Berkeley to excavate in earnest. The fossil beds revealed complete skeletons of the giant ground sloth, mastodon, sabre-tooth cat, and other prehistoric animals.

Orcutt's Rancho Sombra del Roble, now known as Orcutt Ranch, ultimately became the scientist's retirement home. Originally, the property consisted of 210 acres filled with oak trees, a citrus grove, and a creek. Now shrunk to 24 acres, it still offers a taste of what pastoral life was like when pre-industrial Los Angeles was predominantly agricultural land.

At Orcutt, rows of Valencia orange trees rise and spread their old branches, welcoming visitors into their still and peaceful grove. Sweetly scented air hovers thickly, and shady pathways encourage you to wander and slow down the pace. Once ripe, the sweet juicers can be picked on designated dates for a nominal fee. So too can the white grapefruits.

Visitors can also tour the modest white Spanish adobe home and explore the grounds. Of note are the swastikas seen above the windows and doors, on the exterior courtyard floor, and in the ironwork. Before the ancient symbol was co-opted by the Nazis, turning it into a sign of murder and hatred, it was used throughout the world as an emblem of luck and well-being. That is the feeling one carries while taking in the magical surroundings. Surely Orcutt would be pleased. Over the fireplace mantel is the family's slogan: "Mean well, Speak well and Do well."

Address 23600 Roscoe Boulevard, West Hills, CA 91304, Tel +1 818.346.7449, www.laparks.org/dos/horticulture/orcuttranch.htm, orcuttranch.rental@lacity.org | Parking Free on-site lot | Hours Daily, sunrise to sunset | Tip Gobble up some delicious empanadas at Johnny Pacific, just five miles away (7574 Winnetka Avenue, Los Angeles, CA 91306).

76 The Original Los Angeles Subway Terminal

Lost but not forgotten

Car culture rules Los Angeles today, but once upon a time, the city was dominated by public transportation. In fact, tracks for both the Red Cars (long-distance street cars and interurban cars) and Yellow Cars (neighborhood trolleys) crisscrossed the city, connecting them to Long Beach, Santa Monica, Pasadena, and other counties.

But LA residents of the 1920s still yearned for even more public transit to ease traffic congestion. That's when the idea of a subway was hatched. After much contention, the underground tunnel was finally built and opened in December 1925.

The subway tunnel was short – just about a mile – taking passengers between Downtown Los Angeles and the intersection of First Street and Glendale Boulevard. At its peak of usage in the 1940s, commuters were able to shave off up to 20 minutes of their journey, depending on how thick traffic was. It cost about $4 million to build and it shut down a mere 20 years later, as those newfangled things called cars were getting a grip on the LA lifestyle, thanks to what many believe was the manipulation of business tycoons.

On the train's last run, in June 1955, the car bore a banner saying, "To Oblivion." Luckily, the subway was not completely forgotten. A block of it still exists, though currently condemned, between Olive Street and Grand Avenue. The former subway terminal building is now Metro 417 apartments. According to *LA* magazine, developer Forest City Enterprises hopes to renovate the lobby and the loading platforms beneath. During its heyday, the building housed 250,000 square feet of office space and was filled with natural light.

You can walk over the engraved stone in front of Metro 417 that reads, "SVBWAY TERMINAL," and imagine a time when LA's hustle bustle went underground.

Address Engraving is located on the sidewalk in front of 417 S Hill Street, Los Angeles, CA 90013 | **Public transport** Metro Red or Purple Metro Line to Pershing Square Station, then a .1-mile walk | **Parking** Paid lots and metered street parking | **Hours** Engraving always viewable. Note: the Metro 417 building is not open to the public; viewable from the street only. | **Tip** About a block away is the century-old Grand Central Market (317 S Broadway, Los Angeles, CA 90013), where visitors can browse an array of down-home to high-end eateries in a farmers' market-style atmosphere.

77__Pasadena City College Flea Market

Trash and treasure

Since 1977, Pasadena City College Flea Market has brought typically quirky goods, both new and used, to the adventurous buyer. Less well known than its much larger Pasadena competitor, the Rose Bowl Flea Market, the City College fair charges no admission – saving you extra dollars to spend on that special find of the day.

The first Sunday of the month, with a few exceptions each year when the market is closed for holidays, more than 450 vendors assemble in the eastern parking lot, spreading out over three levels of the Bonnie Avenue covered garage known as Lot 5, as well as the open parking lot on the west side of campus. Artfully curated kaleidoscopic wares, mixed with an occasional haphazard jumble of odds and ends, sparkle and tantalize the eye. There's antique furniture, Japanese kakemono with calligraphy and *sumi-e* ink drawings, antique wooden soda boxes, classic vinyl, vintage to contemporary clothing, jewelry, hats, toys, kantha quilts, succulent plants, collectibles of all kinds, and much more. A great treasure is bound to be discovered, and the people-watching is always a treat.

As with all flea markets, arrive early for best finds. But don't sweat it if you've slept in and are still seeking a Sunday adventure. Latecomers can enjoy the beautiful displays and drive a hard bargain for the items vendors don't want to pack up and take home.

As if finding the perfect couch for your home or a pair of thigh-high white go-go boots wasn't enough, a portion of the market's proceeds provides scholarships to Pasadena City College students and helps fund student-led events, a tradition that was started when the fair was founded, and continues to this day.

Food is available for purchase: sweet and savory cobblers, soda, doughnuts. Parking is only $2 (the first bargain of the day).

Address Pasadena City College, 1570 E Colorado Boulevard, Pasadena, CA 91106, Tel +1 626.585.7906, www.pasadena.cdu/fleamarket, fleamarket@pasadena.edu | **Public transport** Gold Line to Allen Station, then a .6-mile walk | **Parking** Paid on-site lots and unmetered street parking | **Hours** First Sunday of the month, 8am–3pm; closed for certain holidays; check website for calendar. | **Tip** Can't wait for the first Sunday of the month to get your secondhand fix? Check out Acts Thrift Store (1382 Locust Avenue, Pasadena CA 91106) for great furniture and clothing finds with daily inventory updates Monday through Saturday (closed Sunday).

78__Pasadena Model Railroad Club

A giant miniature world

Called "Dribblers" because they left a trail of water behind, the first model trains – invented in England in the mid-1800s – were steam powered. Tinkerers soon figured out how to eliminate the mess by using clockwork mechanisms to make the trains move instead. A German toymaker, Marklin, created the first wind-up train that ran on a track. In the early 1900s, an American company, Lionel, produced brightly colored electric-powered trains – setting the standard for model railroaders. It was a keen marketing move when Lionel convinced department stores to display its train sets under Christmas trees, and an iconic image took root.

Founded in 1941, the Pasadena Model Railroad Club celebrates this time-honored hobby by holding regular meetings for its members, who have been building, maintaining, and modernizing the club's 5,000-square-foot model railway system for more than 75 years. The Sierra Pacific Lines, as the railroad is called, claims to be one of the biggest HO layouts in the world. Most members have a certain expertise in modeling, from constructing scenery and train cars to electronics and tech.

The display room is dazzling. Laid out before you is an intricate and vast miniature world, duplicating, to scale and speed, various passenger and freight trains on more than five miles of track. It takes 45 minutes for a train to travel from Alhambra to Zion. The detailed landscape is reflective of West Coast terrain, featuring redwood trees, mountains, and lakes. There's a harbor with ships, a power plant, and a logging area. Each train has a purpose; one carries grain from the fields to the silos, while another transports mail. Surprises abound in this marvelously detailed Lilliputian world. Keep your eyes peeled for the nudist colony, the Bates Motel, and a bear chasing a man up a tree.

Address 5458 Alhambra Avenue, Los Angeles, CA 90032, Tel +1.323.222.1718, www.pmrcc.org, webbmaster@pmrrc.org | **Parking** Unmetered street parking | **Hours** Members meetings: first Tue of the month 7:30pm–10pm, Sat 1pm–5pm. Nonmembers are welcome during meetings, but must call ahead to arrange a visit. Open houses occur in the fall and spring; check website for upcoming dates. | **Tip** Visit the Trina Turk outlet store (1030 Mission Street, South Pasadena, CA 91030), just a few miles away. Loaded with Turk's designer duds at discounted prices, the shop is a bargain hunter's Shangri-la.

79__Peace Awareness Labyrinth & Gardens

Find your self

Penniless and uneducated, Italian-born Secundo Guasti immigrated to Los Angeles in 1878. He managed to save enough money working in restaurants to buy a piece of desert land in Cucamonga, convinced a vineyard would grow. His gamble paid off. By the early 20th century, his was the largest vineyard in the state of California. On his property he built a church, a school, a post office, and homes for all his laborers. He named his "town" Guasti. With his riches, he also commissioned a grand mansion in Los Angeles. The stunning colonial home and its grounds are now owned by the Peace Awareness Labyrinth and Gardens (PALG).

The labyrinth at PALG is designed after the labyrinth at Chartres Cathedral in France, built in about 1220. Made of travertine marble, it's approximately 40 feet across. The path you walk (in and out), totals about a third of a mile. Unlike mazes, which contain impasses and disorienting switchbacks to fool your senses, labyrinths consist of one delineated but serpentine path, leading to a single destination, intended to offer clarity or relief to your mind and spirit.

There are myriad ways to experience the moving meditation. You can simply focus on your breath, or use the path to let go of worry or a burden. If a question is weighing on you, try walking the labyrinth in contemplation of an answer – maybe it will come to you immediately, or in a few days or weeks. Whatever your purpose, it's a sweet time to be alone with yourself.

Labyrinths, both ancient and modern, are considered sacred places where walkers can experience an infinite number of reactions. (No reaction is a fair reaction too.) The one at the PALG is meant to uplift and nourish. The only way out is to retrace your steps, ending at the beginning or beginning at the end – that's for you to decide.

Address 3500 W Adams Boulevard, Los Angeles, CA 90018, Tel +1 323.737.4055, www.peacelabyrinth.org, registrar@peacelabyrinth.org | **Parking** Free on-site lot | **Hours** Call for an appointment to visit the labyrinth. | **Tip** Follow the yellow brick road to dine at the Culver Hotel (9400 Culver Boulevard, Culver City, CA 90232), where the actors who played munchkins in *The Wizard of Oz* stayed while shooting the classic film.

80__Philippe's
Send in the clowns!

Philippe's opened its doors in Los Angeles in 1908. According to company lore, founder Philippe Mathieu made the first French dip when he accidentally dropped a French roll into a pan of au jus and served it up to a local policeman who was in a hurry. The cop returned with hungry friends in search of more "dipped" sandwiches, and so a culinary legend was born. Philippe's relocated to its current location on Alameda Street in 1951 when the 101 freeway came through. And although Mathieu sold the business in 1928, Philippe's remains a family-owned restaurant serving the same classic fare of flaky-crust French dips made with sliced roasted meats, spicy mustard, and purple pickled hardboiled eggs on the side.

Communal seating allows for interesting dining mates, whether they be LA's finest, fans from Dodger's Stadium, neighboring China-town locals, downtown artists, or the general mishmash of humanity that makes Angelenos. Line up at any one of the ten stations at the big front counter, and a so-called carver will pull together your order, serve it up on a paper plate and send you shuffling over the sawdust floor, loaded tray in hand, to find a seat. You'll find beer and wine, including a selection from Los Angeles's San Antonio Winery (see p. 178), on the menu as well.

Long red-topped tables with wooden stools line the front room of Philippe's, while booths are available in the back, where the walls are lined with pictures of clowns and circuses. In the 1940s, veteran Happytime Circus man Paul Eagles started going to Philippe's every Monday. Soon, fellow clowns and circus performers began joining him, launching a tradition that lasted for more than four decades, well into the 1980s. The Big Top veterans no longer meet, but the photos and memorabilia pay tribute to their carnival legacy. Who knew there were so many carnies in the area? Enough to pack the back room at Philippe's.

Address 1001 N Alameda Street, Los Angeles, CA 90012, Tel +1 213.628.3781, www.philippes.com, customerservice@philippes.com | **Public transport** Gold Line to Chinatown Station, then a .3-mile walk | **Parking** Free on-site lot and metered street parking | **Hours** Daily 6am–10pm | **Tip** The Los Angeles Railroad Heritage Foundation maintains a rotating exhibit of miniature trains in the back room of Philippe's.

81 __Plaza

Where machismo is a wallflower

Tony Colpera is the director of the Friday- and Saturday-night shows at Plaza nightclub. When asked if his performers identified as female or male, the white-sequined-T-shirt-clad Colpera replied with a laugh, "They identify as drag queens." He went on to say they are boys by day and girls by night.

Historically speaking, the term "drag queen" likely came about from the hoop skirts worn in the 18th century that dragged on the ground. The derogatory term "queen," meant to describe homosexuals, is thought to have originated in the 19th century, owing to the affected speech of both royalty and gay men. In general, a modern-day drag queen is not transgender or transvestite – but a man who dresses up as a woman for the purposes of performance and entertainment.

Plaza lets visitors experience a micro-culture unique to Los Angeles. The nightclub has been around for 40 years and for most of that time the stage has been graced by not just drag queens, but specifically Latino drag queens. This bears mentioning, since being perceived as gay in what's known to be a very machismo culture can be tough at best and life-threatening at worst. (Latinos and LGBTQ are top recipients of hate crimes in LA, according to the 2014 Los Angeles Hate Crime Report.)

The performers are earnest and put on a very committed show, full of hyper-feminine, glamorous gusto, strutting in front of sparkly curtains. The club is spacious, with an unusually long wooden bar. The musical choices range from Latino love songs to 1970s pop. While the music can be raucous, the crowd tends to be chill and full of both men and women. Audience members sip on incredibly reasonably priced drinks, and with the cash saved, might slip a bill or two into the ladies' tops. Many of the performers have day jobs at fast-food chains, but come nightfall, they transform themselves into sequined, made-up, exuberant divas.

Address 739 N La Brea Avenue, Los Angeles, CA 90038, Tel +1 323.939.0703 | **Parking** Metered and unmetered street parking | **Hours** Daily 9pm–2am; shows at 10:15pm & midnight except Tue & Wed | **Tip** There's nothing like late-night eating in LA. Grab a hot dog at the iconic Hollywood food stand, Pink's (709 N La Brea Avenue, Los Angeles, CA 90039), just a few doors down from Plaza.

82__Poketo at the Line Hotel

Art for your everyday

Poketo, an art project started by Angie Myung and Ted Vadakan in 2003, morphed into a lifestyle brand company with two stores in Los Angeles. Myung and Vadakan originally came up with the concept of sharing the artwork of their talented friends, many in the early stages of their careers, by using affordable plastic and paper wallets as a medium; each priced at about a Jackson.

But they didn't want to just be a wallet company; Poketo hoped to fill people's lives with art and design, whether through beautiful and functional products or meaningful experiences. The company grew slowly and steadily, expanding into areas like housewares, stationery, and apparel. In 2012, Poketo opened a 4,000-square-foot brick-and-mortar shop in the Downtown Los Angeles arts district. Along with curated design goods, they created an event space for workshops, art openings, and cultural happenings to expand on Poketo's mandate to promote art "for the everyday" and share the creative knowledge of artists, musicians, and entrepreneurs.

The renowned boutique hotel purveyor Sydell Group approached Poketo about opening up a space at the glammy modern Line Hotel in Koreatown. Since then, Poketo has been hosting workshops in a suite there, and on sunny days, sometimes in the garden area, with snacks and refreshments provided by Roy Choi's downstairs cafe.

What can you expect at a Poketo workshop? The unexpected. Classes have included making summer sandals, basic techniques for baking a cake that is anything but basic, cocktail mixology, stop-motion animation, paper flower design, mobile phone photography, printmaking, and even an off-site overnighter in Joshua Tree with Los Angeles textile company Block Shop. New workshops are constantly being offered, each promising interesting participants, great conversation, and a hands-on way to connect with the city's creative side.

Address The Line Hotel, 3515 Wilshire Boulevard, Los Angeles, CA 90010, Tel +1 213.381.7411 ext. 3076, www.poketo.com/collections/workshops, poketostore@poketo.com | **Public transport** Purple Line to Wilshire / Normandie Station; the Line Hotel is across the street | **Parking** Valet parking for workshop attendees at a reduced rate of $10; metered street parking | **Hours** Workshops are held on weekends, primarily Saturdays. Times vary; see website for schedule. | **Tip** The Commissary, next to the pool at the Line Hotel, is a beautiful greenhouse setting for breakfast, lunch, dinner, or drinks.

83 __ Royal Palms Beach Tide Pools

Down by the sea

San Pedro is frequently overlooked for its tonier cousin Rancho Palos Verdes. Yet the tide pools at San Pedro's Royal Palms Beach Park are not to be missed.

West of Terminal Island and Point Fermin, curving down to the sea around the coastal mountain holding San Pedro's hillside community of South Shores, Royal Palms Beach sits in a wide cove split into three main areas. Surfers tend to claim the far western section with a few adventurous and perhaps foolhardy riders in the rocky-bottomed center zone. Far west and east, low tide reveals the charcoal-colored rocks pitted with holes bored by piddock clams. Larger rocks in the eastern section of the tide pool break the waves, often with a spectacular plume of ocean spray accompanied by the screams of unsuspecting waders. Commonsense warning: keep away from the edges of rocks where the waves crash; chances are you won't be swept out to sea, but the sharp rocks are sure to do a number on gentle flesh.

Intermittent pools left by the receding tide reveal many purplish anemones. Boulders rise above the pools covered with clinging blue and gray mussels. Hard-shelled striped chitons look like loners by comparison, periodically marking the wet boulders. Trails of tubular marine worm shells can be seen coiled and stretched out like fossils over the rocks. What you won't find at the Royal Palms Beach Park are a lot of people.

The namesake Royal Palms are at the western section of the park in three regal rows with a Copacabana-esque sidewalk installed around them and a line of sturdy picnic tables. The park offers restrooms and a beachside playground for children, but no food. From almost any vantage point you'll have a fantastic view of Santa Catalina Island, just 22 miles from the coast.

Address Royal Palms Beach, 1799 Paseo del Mar, San Pedro, CA 90731,
Tel +1 310.305.9503 | Parking Paid on-site lot. Scaled pricing: 6am–9am & 4pm–close,
$3; 9am–4pm, $8 | Hours Daily 6am–dusk. In winter, parking lot opens at 8am. | Tip The
102-acre White Point Nature Preserve (1600 West Paseo Del Mar, San Pedro, CA 90731)
offers dog-friendly trails above the bluffs with a fantastic view of Santa Catalina.

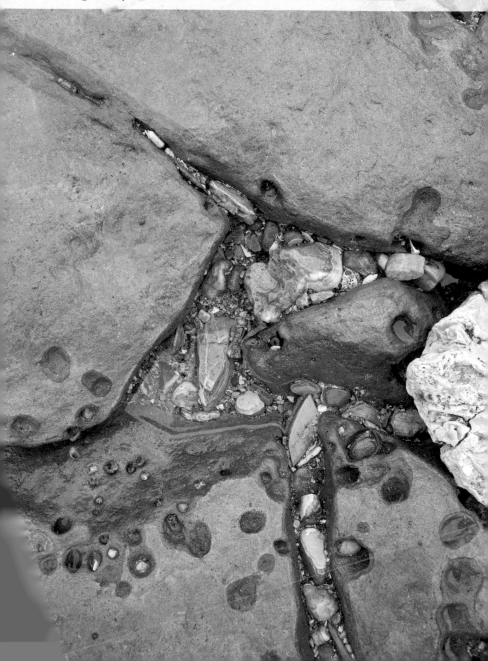

84__Runyon Canyon

A walk above it all

Despite being sandwiched between the bustling flats of Hollywood on the south and the 101 freeway to the north, Runyon Canyon offers 160 acres of wilderness and some of the best views of Los Angeles down to the ocean.

If the canyon could talk, it might tell tales of the capture of the nefarious bandit Tiburcio Vasquez, who was housed and then betrayed by the first land grant holder of Runyon Canyon, "Greek George" Caralambo. Or perhaps the canyon prefers the more salacious stories of the debaucherous parties thrown by Errol Flynn, glamorously homeless after losing his nearby Mulholland estate due to back alimony payments. Flynn briefly took up residence in world-famous Irish tenor John McCormack's pool house (the stone foundation remains are still visible). Architects Frank Lloyd Wright and son Lloyd Wright even developed a plan for an elaborate luxury community here that never came to fruition due to ardent neighborhood opposition.

From the northern Mulholland gate take the left trail for a moderate hike to Clouds Rest, where you can sit and catch your breath on a tall green bench and let your legs dangle like a small kid at the dinner table as you take in the sweeping vista. But the best part of the climb comes halfway up on the left, where perhaps Los Angeles's luckiest goats are corralled next to the trail before a spectacular view of the Hollywood sign and Griffith Observatory to the northeast.

Following the entire loop, depending on personal fitness and the season (winter and spring are typically best, as summer and fall can be blazingly hot), takes anywhere from 90 minutes to two hours; longer if you're really decrepit or lazy – or having too much fun ogling the hiker's butt in front of you. And there are plenty of pretty people in Runyon Canyon to gawk at. The tony nearby estates house some of Los Angeles's most telegenic residents, who like to hike the trail too.

Address North entrance: Mulholland Drive at Desmond Estates Road/Pyramid Place; South entrance: 2000 N Fuller Avenue, Los Angeles, CA 90046 | Parking North entrance: free lot off Mulholland on Pyramid Place/Desmond Estates Road and unmetered street parking; South entrance: unmetered street parking | Hours Daily, dawn to dusk | Tip Mulholland Drive at Cahuenga Boulevard West (Los Angeles, CA 90068) is the eastern terminus of the 21-mile scenic drive that leads to Leo Carillo State Beach.

85_San Antonio Winery

Prohibition survivor

When Stefano Riboli first saw the beautiful Maddalena Satragni, she was sitting atop her family's tractor. Riboli had cruised over in his car, which had an antenna bearing a raccoon tail – quite fashionable at the time. His style screamed "city slicker" – not Satragni's type – or so she thought. Seventy years later, the two are still going strong.

Riboli had moved from Italy to America in 1936, joining the large community of Italians that had settled in the Lincoln Heights neighborhood of Los Angeles. His uncle, Santo Cambianica, put him to work at his almost 20-year-old business, the San Antonio Winery. Back when the winery opened, in 1917, there had been thriving vineyards spread throughout LA, the San Gabriel Valley, and San Bernardino County. But in 1920, Prohibition struck, decimating the region's winemaking industry. Yet, San Antonio survived. Why? The Archdiocese of Los Angeles hired the devoutly Catholic Cambianica to produce sacramental wine.

The ability to evolve and embrace new opportunities has been the key to San Antonio's longevity. For instance, when it became illegal to process whole grapes on the premises and business was threatened, Maddalena hatched a plan to turn the deli into a full-blown cafeteria-style restaurant. Bearing her name, it became the first restaurant in California to open in a winery. Today, the eatery serves up tasty Italian food in rooms lined with redwood casks.

Visitors can tour the winery for free any day of the week. Inhale the tasting room's aromatic scent emanating from its ceiling, which is made of recycled redwood planks used in the original fermentation tanks. Enter the bottling room and witness the wines clinking down a conveyer belt as they are labeled and packed.

Despite his profession, Stefano has never had more than two glasses of red wine at night. After that, the 94-year-old says, "you feel it in your knees. That's when you have to stop."

Address 737 Lamar Street, Los Angeles, CA 90031, Tel , +1 323.223.1401, www.sanantoniowinery.com | Parking Free on-site lot and unmetered street parking | Hours Tours: Mon–Fri noon–4pm on the hour, Sat & Sun 11am–5pm on the hour; Maddalena Restaurant: Sun–Thu 10:30am–6pm, Fri & Sat 10:30am–7pm; Tasting room and gift shop: Sun–Thu 9am–7pm, Fri & Sat 9am–8pm | Tip Visit the very cool art gallery Hauser, Wirth & Schimmel (901 E 3rd Street, Los Angeles, CA 90013).

86 — Santa Anita Stables & Jockey Clubhouse

Follow in the hoofsteps of Seabiscuit

Known as the home of Triple Crown winners Seabiscuit and American Pharoah, the Santa Anita Park racetrack owns a prestigious place in horseracing history. Few know that a free behind-the-scenes tour of the track is offered on Saturday and Sunday mornings during racing season. Advance reservations are required, although it's also wise to arrive 15 minutes prior to departure or risk losing your seats to the ticketless early birds.

Mornings at the track see a group of smiling bettors with briefcases meandering the grounds, while the gorgeous high-strung thoroughbreds work out, the sound of the their muffled hooves on the sand track beating through the air. Technically known as the Seabiscuit Tour (sorry American Pharoah), the excursion begins west of the grandstand in the small parking lot adjacent to the outdoor cafe, Clockers Corner (favorite menu items: coffee, *Daily Racing Form*, cigarettes).

Smart tour goers bring friends and pack the 8:30am tour (which is canceled if fewer than ten people show up). The "tram" heads past the gap where the horses enter and exit the track and meanders through the network of forest-green stables, which feels like a rural equine city. More than 1800 horses train at Santa Anita, and 600-plus people live at the stables, providing around-the-clock care.

The tour ends with a walk that follows the horses' steps from stable to track, and a visit to the jockeys' clubhouse. Entering through the clubhouse's side door, visitors pass through the silks room, where the jockeys' brightly colored jerseys hang wall-to-wall on pegs. The silks room opens to a small workout area that includes a mechanical horse. Deeper into the clubhouse, jockeys lounge in their robes next to lockers, some topped with rows of riding boots in a rainbow of colors.

Address Santa Anita Park, 285 W Huntington Drive, Arcadia, CA 91007, Tel +1 626.574.7223, www.santaanita.com, info@santaanita.com | Public transport Gold Line to Arcadia Station, then a .8-mile walk | Parking Free lot at Gate 8 off Baldwin Avenue | Hours Tours: Sat & Sun 8:30am & 9:45am by reservation only, call +1 626.574.6677. Track hours vary; open during racing season, Dec–June; check www.santaanita.com/full-calendar for details. | Tip Zelo Pizzeria (324 E Foothill Boulevard, Arcadia, CA 91006), less than two miles away, offers a cornmeal-crust pizza that will break your heart and delight your taste buds.

87 __ Santa Fe Dam Recreation Area

Dam it all

The Santa Fe Dam Recreational Area – despite its immense size – is a hidden gem in San Gabriel Valley. It's like something an overzealous recreation-loving uncle would construct, especially if he worked for the Army Corp of Engineers in 1947, when the dam (after which the park is named) was completed. This park has it all: play structures made of rope that look like a giant spiderweb, a water play area, swim beach, year-round fishing, nonmotorized boating, biking, trees, birding, hiking, picnic spots with charcoal grills, equestrian trails, a nature center, and so much more. No booze permitted, though. The rec area is dry when it comes to alcohol.

But it was anything but dry in 1938, when two storms came in quick succession heading east toward the San Gabriel Mountains, dumping 10 inches of rain over a period of six days. The resulting flood swept through Los Angeles and pooled in Orange, Riverside, and San Bernardino Counties, wiping out entire communities. The flood inspired the creation of the Santa Fe Dam and the channeling of the rivers to curtail such calamity in the future.

The 836-acre mixed-use park sits in the Santa Fe Flood Control Basin and is home to a 70-acre lake with three islands. In the summer months, paddleboats, rowboats, and kayaks are available for rent. Visitors are welcome to bring their own nonmotorized boats, although there is a launching fee. Bring a bike to enjoy the miles of cycling paths that go through and around the park, or rent a surrey on-site.

A cordoned-off swim area and beach dotted with blue-and-white lifeguard stations is open seasonally. Pretty stellar bird watching, especially for waterfowl, happens year-round, with a guided bird walk the third Saturday of each month, free of charge.

Address 15501 E Arrow Highway, Irwindale, CA 91706, Tel +1 626.334.1065, www.parks.lacounty.gov (click on "Parks Locator" and search "Santa Fe Dam Recreation Area"), info@parks.lacounty.gov | **Parking** On-site lot; $10 vehicle entry charge | **Hours** Nov 1–Apr 30, daily 6:30am–6pm; May 1–Oct 31, daily 6:30am–8pm. Children's water play area open from Memorial Day to Labor Day; $2/person/90-minute session. Swim area open Memorial Day through June, weekends only; July through Labor Day, Thu–Sun | **Tip** Every weekend for one month in the spring, a portion of the park is transformed into a Medieval township during the Original Renaissance Pleasure Faire. Visit www.renfaire.com/socal for exact dates and prices.

88 The Schindler House

Quintessential California living

The home of Rudolph Schindler and his wife, Pauline, in West Hollywood is considered by many to be the first modernist house. Using affordable concrete, a signature element of the modernist design movement, the Schindler House's walls were cast on-site then tilted into place, barn-raising style, by crane.

Schindler designed the Kings Road house as a co-residence for he and Pauline and another family, Clyde and Marian DaCamara Chace. Clyde worked as an engineer for architect Irving Gill. Marian and Pauline were friends from their days at Smith College. The idea was to create an experimental communal residence with separate, private living areas and shared kitchen. Unlike typical homes of the day, the Schindler House was built without a conventional dining area or bedrooms. Occupants retiring for the evening would climb stairs to the rooftop's so-called sleeping baskets, which were protected by a tentlike tarp but open to the elements.

With giant apartment and condominium complexes dwarfing the Schindler House today, it may be difficult to picture what the site looked like in 1922, when the house was built and LA's landscape was open and undeveloped. Back then there were distant horizons uninterrupted by visual clutter, with a wide view of the San Gabriel Mountains. Imagine the ability to pull a long table out of the house and dine al fresco next to Frank Lloyd Wright and his son, to pour a glass of wine for John Cage, or to sit with Edward Weston and talk about his latest photography project. Imagine the home radiating warm light, the tinkle of silverware, and the bubbling sounds of laughter and camaraderie. Modern living at its best.

Oddly, Schindler's work on his own home went largely unnoticed by the architectural establishment during his lifetime. It was only after his death, in 1953, that the innovations of his design gained greater recognition.

Address 835 N Kings Road, West Hollywood, CA 90069, Tel +1 323.651.1510, MAKcenter.org, office@MAKcenter.org | Parking Paid lot at Kings Road and Santa Monica Boulevard; unmetered street parking | Hours Wed–Sun 11am–6pm, closed Mon–Tue. Admission: $7 general, $6 students & seniors, free on Fri 4pm–6pm. | Tip The catfish po'boy with thin lemon slices at the Gumbo Pot (6333 W 3rd Street, Suite 312, Los Angeles, CA 90036) in the Farmers Market at 3rd and Fairfax is well worth the parking hassle created by the neighboring Grove shopping center.

89__ Serra Springs

Where sacred waters still flow

There is something amazing about looking down and seeing water bubbling up from the ground, especially in the middle of a giant, developed city. But there it is, ceaselessly gurgling, since at least the fifth century, pumping an astonishing 22,000 to 25,000 gallons of water a day into the ocean.

The ancient waters of Serra Springs have seen a lot of action. Researchers of all backgrounds are still trying to piece together exactly how the springs were used. It's a bit of a guessing game, since much of the culture and language of the Gabrielino/Tongva, the first people who inhabited the Los Angeles basin, has not survived colonization. It's thought that a village called Kuruvunga was located near the springs. It's also thought that it was some type of meeting place, where various nations could trade, rest, and drink deeply of the fresh water. Because Father Junipero Serra supposedly said mass there, the Spaniards named the site after him. One thing is for certain, skeletons and precious objects have been excavated, leading people to believe the land around the springs, including that on which University High School sits, is a burial ground, and therefore considered sacred.

In 1992, galvanized by the prospect of the springs being turned into a parking lot, the Gabrielino/Tongva Foundation, made up of politicians, citizens, Uni High students, and Native Americans, was founded with the aim of restoring the springs' natural habitat, educating the public, and preserving the history of the native culture that once thrived there.

Peace descends while sitting or walking among the plants and trees that populate the area. Weeds rule here, making the environment feel wild and untouched. Lots of birds happily sing. And that primeval spring, still flowing, indifferent to the changes swirling around it, is quite a sight to see.

Address Located off an alley next to 1415 Stoner Avenue, Los Angeles, CA 90025,
Tel +1 310.806.2418, www.gabrielinosprings.com, program@gabrielinosprings.com | Parking
Unmetered street parking | Hours First Sat of every month, 10am–3pm. Call first to arrange a
visit. | Tip Zip over to the nearby Hammer Museum (10899 Wilshire Boulevard, Los Angeles,
CA 90024), featuring founder Armand Hammer's classic art collection, as well as a growing
collection of cutting-edge contemporary art with an LA-centric focus.

90 __ Shumei Retreat House

From literary nest to spiritually blessed

Hollywood writing royalty Joan Didion and husband Gregory Dunne lived in a big quasi-Georgian home with a Spanish-style twist on Franklin Avenue from 1967 to 1971. In Didion's book *The White Album*, she reminisces about those freewheeling, anti-anxiety-pill-popping days, with many houseguests, open doors, and daughter Quintana Roo playing tennis on the court in the backyard. They hosted parties attended by Hollywood luminaries, among them Janis Joplin, who would later die of an overdose in a hotel room down the street, in 1970. The house belonged Dunne's uncle. There, Didion wrote *Play It as It Lays* and her seminal essay collection *Slouching Towards Bethlehem*.

In 1979, Shumei bought the building, opening its first western outpost. Shumei is influenced by the ancient religions of Shinto, Buddhism, Christianity, as well as Western philosophy. It is based on a spiritual practice of chanting, Natural Agriculture, celebrating art and beauty in everyday life, and sharing *Jyorei*, a healing art that promotes health, happiness, and well-being. The public is welcome to join daily morning and evening chanting, called *sampai*.

The Shumei Retreat House also maintains a demonstration garden in its backyard, full of completely chemical- and pesticide-free fruits and vegetables. Open during daylight hours, it is an integral part of its commitment to Natural Agriculture, a method that embraces harmony between nature and humanity.

Fava beans and black soybeans grow in neat rows on the site of the former tennis court, which took master gardener Junzo Uyeno four years to excavate. A rototiller couldn't break the compacted earth; so, he patiently dug three feet into the ground, working with the soil to transform it into the fertile and prolific garden it is today. The retreat house offers gardening workshops and work-exchange programs for food cultivated in the garden.

Address 7406 Franklin Avenue, Los Angeles, CA 90046, Tel +1 213.876.5528, www.shumei.us/hollywood, hollywood@shumei.us | **Public transport** Red Line to Hollywood and Highland Station, then a .9-mile walk | **Parking** Small on-site lot and unmetered street parking | **Hours** Daily chanting: 9am & 7pm, by reservation only. Demonstration garden: open during daylight hours. | **Tip** Meltdown Comics (7522 Sunset Boulevard, Los Angeles, CA 90046), just over a half mile away, has a fantastic selection of independent comics and superhero staples with rotating art exhibits.

91 Silent Movie Theatre
[Scream!]

Some say the Silent Movie Theatre is star crossed and haunted. John Hampton built the picture house from scratch, transforming an open lot on Fairfax into the theater of his dreams, opening in 1942. As movie studios turned to talkies, many of the silent films suffered from classic Hollywood indifference and were destroyed intentionally or through neglect and improper storage. Hampton preserved his growing collection of celluloid silent films by immersing them in toxic chemicals in the bathtub of his apartment above the theater. Ultimately, his efforts may have contributed to his demise; he died of cancer in 1990.

Lawrence Austin, a friend of John and his wife, Dorothy Hampton, took over proprietorship of the theater in 1991. He brought in an organist to provide live accompaniment to the films. Prior to each screening, the organist would play "Pomp and Circumstance" as Austin strode to the front of the auditorium to deliver an erudite introduction to the evening's film.

Six years later, after delivering such an opening address, on January 17, 1997, Austin returned to the lobby and was gunned down and killed. Also shot was teenage ticket taker and concessionaire Mary Giles, who survived her wounds to identify her assailant and Austin's killer: 19-year-old Christian Rodriguez. Subsequent testimony revealed Rodriguez was a gun-for-hire on behalf of Austin's lover and projectionist James Van Sickle, the lone beneficiary of the theater should Austin die. Both were convicted of murder, barely escaping the death penalty, and are serving life sentences for their crime.

Subsequent owner Charlie Lustman claimed to have heard the ghostly jangling of pocket change, a habit of the late Austin, in the empty lobby. The Cinefamily took over in 2007 and now hosts private events and screenings with celebrity guests, and shows art films and, on occasion, silent movies.

Address The Cinefamily at the Silent Movie Theatre, 611 N Fairfax Avenue, Los Angeles, CA 90036, Tel +1 323.655.2510, www.cinefamily.org, info@cinefamily.org | **Parking** Metered street parking | **Hours** Mon–Fri 11am–6pm | **Tip** Iconic Canter's Deli (419 N Fairfax Avenue, Los Angeles, CA 90036), just south on Fairfax, serves up a mean matzo ball soup and bagel with schmear 24/7.

92__Skeletons in the Closet
Macabre merch

Face it, it's a grim business at the Los Angeles County Department of Medical Examiner-Coroner. God forbid, you or anyone you know ends up there on official business or with a tag around your cold big toe. Much more lighthearted is a visit to the coroner gift shop, known as Skeletons in the Closet.

Both the coroner's office and the gift shop are housed in an old brick building that originally served as the Los Angeles County Hospital's Administration Building. The stately lobby with black-and-white hexagonal tiles looks like it came straight from central casting. A receptionist sits behind glass in a dark wood booth to the left of the main entrance. Straight ahead is a somberly beautiful staircase with wooden banisters the same hue as the receptionist booth. The dim lighting and dearth of natural light accentuates the solemnity. The overall effect feels like something out of a Raymond Chandler novel, as if Detective Philip Marlowe might step forward any minute and put his hat on as he exits the building.

To the right of the lobby is a wooden framed door with an oversized clouded glass window, that has the words GIFT SHOP written on it in capital letters. The macabre mood lifts somewhat inside the store, which has been in business since 1993, selling official coroner merchandise, like beanies and scrubs, mixed with such droll items as towels with a body chalk line, golf umbrellas, miniature skeletons, temporary tattoos, garment "body" bags, and even plush toy replicas of Indy, the coroner's German shepherd work dog. Indy is slated to retire in 2016 and the tribute doll was made in honor of her years of loyal service. When asked specifically what Indy does, the response from the sales attendant was "Digs up bones." All right then, this is the coroner's office, after all.

Even with the grave reality of the subject at hand, the dark humor of Skeletons in the Closet is something to be enjoyed.

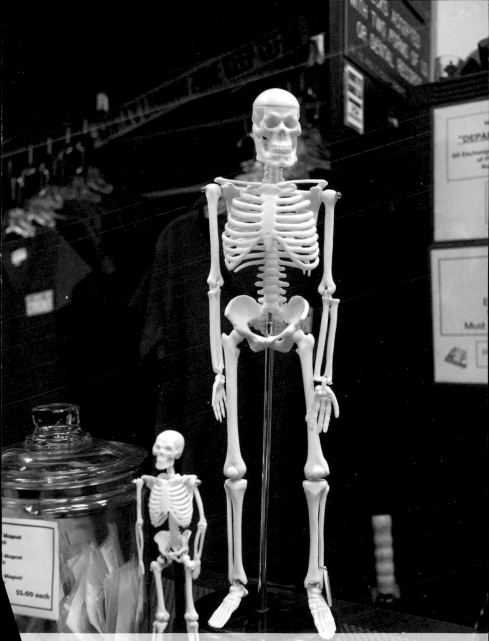

Address 1104 N Mission Road, Los Angeles, CA 90033, Tel +1 323.343.0760,
www.lacoroner.com, giftshop@coroner.lacounty.gov | **Parking** Limited free on-site spaces;
four metered spots on N Mission Road, north side of the street past Sichel Street; paid lot
ast of the coroner's office | **Hours** Mon – Fri 8:30am – 4pm | **Tip** Barbara's at the Brewery
20 Moulton Avenue #110, Los Angeles, CA 90031), in the renowned Brewery Art
lony, offers a wide variety of craft beers on tap.

93__ The Source Restaurant
Peace, love, and sprouts

In the early 1970s, finding a gluten-free, vegan organic lunch wasn't so easy. Enter white-bearded polygamist Father Yod, also known as Jim Baker, and the long-haired Source Family cult, who served up plates of meatless chow supposedly prepared with the highest cosmic frequency. The godfather of fitness, Jack LaLanne, who lived till age 96, ever a finicky and healthful eater who rarely dined out, swore by the meals offered at the Source Restaurant and the other two Baker institutions, the Aware Inn and Old World on Sunset.

Father Yod and the Source Family were legendary on the Sunset Strip. The cult first lived in a beautiful 1914 mansion in Los Feliz owned by the Los Angeles newspaper moguls, the Chandlers; then, when their lease wasn't renewed, they relocated to a much smaller house in Nichols Canyon. Yod was partial to white suits and rolled in a Rolls Royce full of seriously stunning multicultural Source Family beauties who would spill out of the car, their flowing gowns and gorgeous bright faces gleaming. Restaurateur. Spiritual guru. And band leader. Father Yod and the Family also played psychedelic rock music; albums and videos are still available today online.

Everyone came to the Source – from rock icon John Lennon, no less, to movie stars like Goldie Hawn and Warren Beatty. Woody Allen even spoofed the establishment during a scene in *Annie Hall*, in which Allen's character Alvy Singer orders alfalfa sprouts with mashed yeast on the Source patio, after which he causes a commotion in the parking lot when he crashes his car.

The Source sold in 1974, with Yod and the Family relocating to Hawaii, where within a year, Yod would hang glide to the "other side," crashing on the beach and dying days later. Today, the building on the northwest corner of Sunset Boulevard and Sweetzer Avenue is home to Cabo Cantina, and although cosmic frequencies are not on the menu, big margaritas are.

Address Cabo Cantina, 8301 W Sunset Boulevard, West Hollywood, CA 90069, Tel +1 323.822.7820, www.cabocantina.com, cabosunset@thecabocantina.com | **Parking** Paid lots and metered street parking | **Hours** Mon & Wed 4pm–midnight, Tue & Thu 4pm–1:30am, Fri & Sat noon–1:30am, Sun noon–midnight | **Tip** The Chateau Marmont (8221 Sunset Boulevard, Los Angeles, CA 90046), three blocks east on Sunset Boulevard, offers an old-school stylish lobby and bar, and a ton of pretty – and often famous – people.

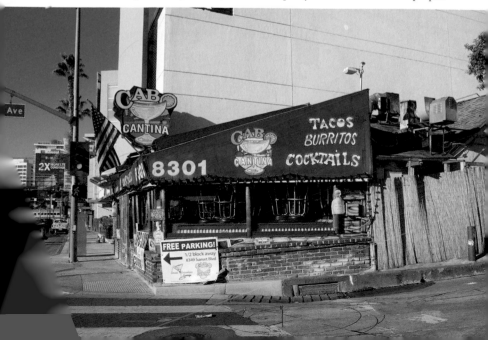

94_ Stoney Point
The boulder approach

In the far northwest region of Los Angeles County in the Valley, an outcropping of picturesque sandstone rocks bubbles over the landscape. These boulders captivated a local Burbank falconer and budding entrepreneur named Yvon Chouinard, who at the age of 15, spent many a weekend, often barefoot, on the Stoney Point crag learning to rock climb and rappel. As a falconer, Chouinard had to be able to lower himself down to aeries using ropes to capture a falcon to train, a practice still used today under strict apprenticeship with the California Hawking Association. Chouinard's early experiences at Stoney Point sparked a lifelong love of the natural world and extreme mountain climbing, which spawned his creation of the successful outdoor equipment and clothing company Patagonia.

But one need not have all that ambition to enjoy the bouldering and hikes at Stoney Point, only a bit of fortitude to park on Topanga Canyon Boulevard to the west and Canoga Avenue to the east. (Exit your car on the non-traffic side for safety.)

Mild hikes can be accessed from almost any starting location and hikers can watch climbers crawl over massive rocks. Or, embrace your inner Chouinard and scale the boulders yourself. The sport of bouldering involves climbing without ropes and harnesses for typically short ascents, often 20 feet or less (we aren't talking free climbing up the face of Half Dome in Yosemite here).

If you'd like a bit of guidance or have a desire to climb and rappel, local REI stores often offer classes for a fee that includes gear – ropes and harnesses for rappelling, optional mats for bouldering, and specifically designed climbing shoes with a softer rubber covering the toe and arch for added grip (visit www. rei.com/learn for more information). But don't be surprised if you see Stoney Point climbers foregoing shoes altogether, just as Chouinard once did.

Pack plenty of water as none is available on-site.

Address Topanga Canyon Boulevard between Canoga Avenue south of 118 Freeway, Chatsworth, CA 91311 | Parking Unmetered street parking on Topanga Canyon Boulevard to the west and Canoga Avenue to the east. Never leave valuables visible in the car. | Hours Daily, sunrise to sunset | Tip Modernist real-estate developer Joseph Eichler built 108 homes from 1963 to 1964 in an area of Granada Hills known as the Balboa Highlands (Balboa Boulevard and Lisette Street, Los Angeles, CA 91344). Drive or walk through the neighborhood to see the signature glass entryways and sloped roofs.

95 Sugihara Sculpture
The power of one

On a bench at the edge of Little Tokyo in Downtown LA sits a man made of bronze, his hand extended. In it is something hard to discern. The inscription next to this unassuming memorial can be hard to read, especially if it's one of those blinding Los Angeles afternoons. But the story of this relatively unknown WWII hero, Chiune Sugihara, demands attention.

Born of humble roots, Sugihara excelled in his studies and rose through government ranks to the position of Japanese Consul-General. In 1939, he was stationed in Lithuania, and was soon confronted with the Nazi invasion of Poland, which sent thousands of terrified Jewish refugees into Lithuania. It would be a short-lived safe haven. A year later, the Germans were closing in, and almost all foreign embassies were evacuated – but not Japan's. Chiune and his wife, Yukiko, moved by the plight of desperate people, asked their government for, and received, a 20-day extension. Thousands of panicked Jews flooded the Japanese embassy, seeking exit visas.

A visa is what the statue of Sugihara holds in its hand. Despite the explicit prohibition of their government, Sugihara and his wife relentlessly handwrote and stamped 300 passports a day, giving permission for Jews to receive safe passage out. It's said Sugihara continued to write visas while leaving the country, and handed his visa stamp through the train window to a Jewish refugee when time ran out, so that the refugee could continue the work. More than 6,000 Jews were saved by the Sugiharas' willingness to risk their lives. At war's end, the Japanese government removed Sugihara from his beloved diplomatic service – for life.

Next to the statue is space enough for a visitor to sit. Perhaps Ramon Velazco, the artist who made the sculpture, wished to offer a place where a person can rest and marvel at the amazing human capacity for bravery and compassion, in the face of tremendous peril.

Address 192 S Central Avenue, Los Angeles, CA 90012 | Public transport Metro Gold Line to Little Tokyo Station, then a .3-mile walk | Parking Metered street parking | Hours Always viewable | Tip In the nearby historic Little Tokyo village, find Mitsuru Café (117 Japanese Village Plaza Mall, Los Angeles, CA 90012), where you can watch fresh *imagawayaki* (a pancake filled with sweet azuki-bean paste) being made.

96_Surfrider Beach

Dude, here rolls the perfect wave

The long crescent shoreline, combined with cobbles and sand supplied by Malibu Creek, makes Surfrider Beach one of the most renowned point breaks in the world. A point break is a wave that breaks onto an obstruction, like rocks. The Surfrider waves rule supreme because of their size and shape. They're about six feet from top to bottom and can provide long rides. It's possible to catch a single wave from Malibu Beach Lagoon all the way to Malibu Pier – about a half mile. Soft enough for beginners to learn on, yet swift and hollow enough for the more advanced to rip, the waves are suitable for surfers of all experience levels. Champions of the sport Andy Lion and Allen Sarlo are seen frequently in the waters here.

During the summer there's a south swell that makes it a popular season for surfing. For weeks, the waters are deliciously warm, often hovering in the 70s – no need for a wetsuit. The wind, if any, is light, preventing the faces of the waves from getting choppy. Anecdotally, the temperature in the cove tends to be 10 degrees higher than the great Zuma Beach, 10 miles to the north. Even a fog bank stretching 13 miles from Zuma south to Big Rock will somehow magically skip Surfrider, leaving the cove endlessly sunny.

Despite being such an idyllic beach, Surfrider was relatively unknown to the world until it was immortalized in the 1959 movie *Gidget*. Based on the book by Frederick Kohner, *Gidget* chronicled the efforts of Kohner's teenage daughter, Kathy, to surf with the boys in Malibu. ("Gidget" was a nickname given to Kathy – a combination of the words "girl" and "midget.")

Find the iconic brick wall, often covered with a row of colorful surfboards, where the character Gidget leaned her board. Located south of the better-known Malibu Lagoon State Beach, it's a great spot to kick it year-round, watching the beach rats compete for that perfect wave.

Address Just south of the Adamson House: 23200 Pacific Coast Highway, Malibu, CA 90265 | **Parking** Unmetered street parking along Pacific Coast Highway; paid lot at Malibu Lagoon State Beach; paid lot next to Adamson House | **Hours** Daily, sunrise to sunset | **Tip** Take a tour of the Adamson House (see address above; www.adamsonhouse.org). Built in 1929, it is the ultimate Malibu beach house, with an old California history.

97__Tam's Burgers #21
Come for the gangsta history, stay for the fries

Tam's on West Rosencrans Avenue has been slinging big burgers since 1971. Simple is the modus operandi at Tam's. The windows are covered in bright decals with oversized pictures of gut-busting menu items like the pastrami burger and chili cheese fries. Over the years the menu has expanded to include Mexican food staples like burritos and tamales alongside classic American diner fare. Dining is available inside at one of nine booths in a long galley-style corridor next to white tiled walls with light blue and red accents, or outside under a green corrugated metal awning at circular cement tables.

Or opt for drive-thru service. Don't be alarmed by the bulletproof glass between the cashier and the customer. Compton, CA, has a storied past. Hard hit by the crippling crack epidemic of the eighties, Compton was plagued by gang violence. It was also the cornerstone of West Coast gangsta rap – giving rise to such hip-hop acts as N.W.A., whose story is brilliantly told in the biopic *Straight Outta Compton*. Consider the bulletproof glass a souvenir of those days. (You can bet your boots the Starbucks across the street wasn't around back then.)

Tam's was the site of an old-school gangsta flashback on a fateful afternoon in late January 2015. Death Row Records cofounder Suge Knight, having allegedly just been asked to leave the set of a TV promo for *Straight Outta Compton* being filmed a few blocks away, rolled into the Tam's parking lot in his red F-150 Raptor truck. A surveillance video captured blurry images of rapper-turned-filmmaker Cle "Bone" Sloan approaching Knight's truck on foot, followed by a flurry of punches exchanged through the driver's-side window, and finally the Raptor backing up over Sloan, exiting the frame, and then returning and running over Terry Carter, a longtime Compton resident with ties to the music biz. A somber episode from Compton's rough past.

Address 1201 W Rosecrans Avenue, Compton, CA 90222, Tel +1 310.537.8478 | **Parking** Free on-site lot | **Hours** Daily 6am–midnight | **Tip** Watts Towers (1727 E 107th Street, Los Angeles, CA 90002), about 3.5 miles north, is the lifelong work of Simon Rodia and an iconic symbol of the Watts neighborhood. Tours are available for a nominal fee Thu–Sat 10:30am to 3pm, Sun noon–3pm).

98__Terminal Annex Murals

Perfectly preserved government-funded art

It took the artist Boris Deutsch about five years to paint the 11 half-circle panels called *Cultural Contributions of North, South and Central America*, in the still-functioning Terminal Annex post office. Completed in 1944, the project was funded by the Treasury Section of Fine Arts, which oversaw the artworks created to enhance public buildings. Compared to the Work Projects Administration (WPA), the goal of which was work relief (thereby resulting in artworks of wide-ranging quality), the Treasury Section chose their artists carefully, through a prestigious competition. Deutsch was among those selected.

Boris Deutsch was born in Lithuania in 1892. Drafted into the Russian Army during World War I, he deserted after realizing he was incapable of killing. After fleeing across Asia, he ultimately ended up in Los Angeles. Shortly after his arrival, he won the Terminal Annex commission.

The first six lunettes depict indigenous people making pottery, weaving, dancing, and playing music, and the surrounding mission of Junipero Serra. The following panel shows people traveling west. The next four abruptly turn to modern day, portraying the 200-inch Hale Telescope, physics class, telephone operators, and military men in "Defense of America."

If you study panels eight through ten, you'll notice a woman who appears in all three. She's the wife of the astronomer, a physics teacher, and also the lady in red in the "Communication" panel. This raven-haired woman is Deutsch's wife, Riva.

Deutsch made his frescoes to last. That meant no oil and no casein. So, he came up with his own solution: egg yolk. He mixed it with a few drops of water and concentrated dry pigment. The concoction worked. It was thin and absorbed into the plaster, therefore there was nothing to crack and flake off. The deep earth tones are as rich today as they were when freshly painted.

Address The US Post Office – Los Angeles Terminal Annex, 900 N Alameda Street, Los Angeles, CA 90012 | **Public transport** Any Metro line to Union Station, then a .2-mile walk | **Parking** Paid on-site lot and metered street parking | **Hours** Mon–Fri 0am–5pm & Sat 9am–1pm | **Tip** Visit the Avila Adobe (10 Olvera Street, Los Angeles, A 90012). Built in 1818, it's the oldest standing residence in Los Angeles, and is open he public as a museum.

99__Time Travel Mart

"Wherever you are, we're already then."

At the Time Travel Mart in Echo Park, you'll find all the wares necessary for the modern-day time traveler. Barbarian repellant (fends off a dozen barbarians at once). Time travel sickness pills. Corinthian, centurion, and conquistador helmets to blend in when voyaging back to an earlier era – or robot milk, if visiting the future. And of course, an official "pastport" (don't attempt intertemporal travel without it). But there's more. The Time Travel Mart is a front for McSweeney's Dave Eggers 826LA writing and tutoring program for area resident kids ages 6 to 18.

Started in San Francisco in 2002, Eggers and educator Nínive Calegari looked for a way to help teachers by tutoring students in typically underserved schools and nurturing their enthusiasm for writing. The original 826 Valencia was zoned retail, so Eggers and Calegari were obligated to include a retail component to their free tutoring service. They went with a pirate theme, self-lauded as San Francisco's "Only Independent Pirate Supply Store," for the flagship. The practice of including a shop with a twist has continued ever since, in all eight national chapters.

Behind the small storefront in Echo Park on Sunset, area students can pass through the time portal hallway to the back room. The portal exit opens to a wide writing space with elevated ceilings, a brick wall along one side, and a floor blanketed with thick wooden worktables encircled by metal Navy side chairs. Beyond the tables, sofas are arranged conversationally in an alcove next to floor-to-ceiling wooden shelves filled with books. A loft area above houses desks for staff. Working writers teach courses on diverse subjects ranging from penning comics to songwriting. Student work is published and available for purchase. You'll find it in the refrigerated section of the Time Travel Mart. Proceeds support 826LA, of course.

Address 1714 W Sunset Boulevard, Los Angeles, CA 90026, Tel +1 213.413.3388, www.timetravelmart.com, info@timetravelmart.com | **Parking** Metered street parking | **Hours** Mon – Sun noon–6pm | **Tip** Sage Vegan Bistro (1700 Sunset Boulcvard, Los Angeles, CA 90026), just steps east of the Time Travel Mart, serves a seasonal menu of delicious vegan food and dairy-free ice cream.

100__Tonga Hut
Return of the killer zombie

It took Jeff "the Beachbum" Berry over a decade to find the original recipe for the 1934 cocktail that set off the tiki craze in Los Angeles and beyond. The libation? The Zombie. The inventor of the recipe was the man who introduced Polynesian kitsch culture to the United States, "Don Beach," born Earnest Raymond Beaumont Gantt. He dabbled in bootlegging toward the end of Prohibition, and then opened a tiki bar in Hollywood in 1933. It was all about rum and escapism. In those days, people couldn't travel much, so visiting Beach's bar felt like a getaway to an exotic land with unusual tastes and wild island décor. Same too, with the Tonga Hut, which hasn't changed much since it opened in 1958. It's very dark, with the ever-present sound of gurgling water. Lovely topless Polynesian ladies adorn the walls over the squishy vinyl booths.

When the Beachbum finally got his hands on the elusive Zombie recipe, he found one component written essentially in code, labeled simply "Don's Mix." Additional sleuthing unearthed the ingredients in Don's Mix, which included "Spices #4." Yet more digging revealed that Spices #4 used to be kept by Beach in a safe in Inglewood. What's up with the hardcore hiding? Back in the days of the tiki explosion, the competition grew to be brutal. Beach only shared his recipes with his most trusted bartenders. But what did Spices #4, the final unknown ingredient, consist of? Eventually, Berry ran into an old bartender of Beach's who shared the secret. It was ... cinnamon syrup.

The current general manager of Tonga Hut learned how to make the original Zombie from Berry. All the ingredients are fresh and unlike the overly sweet bastardized imitations one finds on the menus at "less devoted" bars, the cocktail you'll get at Tonga Hut is authentic. It's a muscular drink with big rum flavor, including traces of anise, lime, clove, and, of course, cinnamon.

Address 12808 Victory Boulevard, North Hollywood, CA 91606, Tel +1 818.769.0708, www.tongahut.com, tongahut@gmail.com | Parking Free on-site lot | Hours Daily 4pm–2am | Tip Dive into Hollywood Cinema history, before you dive into a historical drink, at the Hollywood Museum (1660 Highland Avenue, Los Angeles, CA 90028), where a giant collection of Tinseltown memorabilia is held.

101_ Trapeze School New York

Look Ma, no hands!

The initiated call it flying. The pedestal board stands 23 feet above the pier with the Pacific Ocean underneath, waves rumbling through the pylons below. The world's only solar-powered Ferris wheel spins next door and the roar of the nearby roller coaster drowns out the ocean each time it rushes past. One terrifying step off the board and you're sailing through the salty air with the trapeze bar clenched in hand. Then comes the exhilaration of letting go, taking a literal leap of faith as you reach out to grab the next bar or even the outstretched hands of another person. Talk about a trust exercise.

Trapeze School New York on the Santa Monica Pier offers daily two-hour trapeze classes ranging from novice to "throw and catch" for the advanced aerialist. Not ready to take the big leap off the high board? Trapeze School New York also hosts shorter classes that are closer to the ground – or pier in this case – for aerial silks, static trapeze, hoops, trampoline, and conditioning. Children are welcome provided they have the necessary attention span and focus. If a young flyer peters out midway through a lesson, no problem, but also no refunds.

The instructors are eager to work with all those who want to learn. According to the school, three factors contribute to being an aerialist: weight, body shape, and grip. The trapeze artist aspirant should be able to hang for at least 30 seconds. The safety belt may not fit all body shapes properly and those 205 pounds and heavier enter into what is called the "weight hesitation" zone. Not to worry if that sounds like you; the school promises to devise a plan to help every dedicated but not-ready-for-prime-time flyer realize his or her trapeze dreams.

The school's motto, "Forget fear. Worry about the addiction," is well conceived. One class, and you might just be hooked for life.

Address 370 Santa Monica Pier, Santa Monica, CA 90401, Tel +1 310.394.5800,
losangeles.trapezeschool.com, lainfo@trapezeschool.com | **Public transport** Expo Line to
Downtown Santa Monica Station, then a .5-mile walk | **Parking** Paid lots and metered
street parking | **Hours** Daily 8:30am–10pm, weather permitting | **Tip** Muscle Beach
(1800 Ocean Front Walk, Venice, CA 90291), 2.5 miles south, started in 1934 and has been
home to the workouts of former governor Arnold Schwarzenegger, among many others.

102 VDL Research House II

Ashes to ashes

"Mother, I have very bad news. Our house has burned down." It was March 1963, and the home designed by the great modernist architect Richard Neutra, in which he and his wife, Dione, had raised their three boys, was a fire-ravaged shell. The Neutras were out of town when the electricity short-circuited, or it's likely they would have perished. What few know is that when Dione got the call from her son Dion, she made the tough choice not to share the tragic news with her husband for an entire week, so as not to ruin his trip. According to Dione, Neutra had recently been low in spirits. His son Raymond urged that building a new house up from the ashes was the perfect antidote to his dad's depression.

Neutra and Dion, also an architect, collaborated to rebuild the VDL Research House II. The result, with its floor-to-ceiling windows and sliding glass doors, is an embrace of "nature-near" living – a Neutra hallmark. His designs were a far cry from the Baroque architecture of his native city, Vienna, incorporating modern features and techniques – the use of smooth metal, sleek lines, and natural-light-filled rooms.

There's a tension in Neutra's residence. The rooms are surprisingly small, with low ceilings, and the open staircases are narrow and steep. In contrast, the walls of glass and integration of outdoor patios create a sense of endless – and boundless – space.

The house was constantly crowded. By day, Neutra's draftsmen lived and worked on the first floor – alongside their boss. By night, the couple regularly entertained, staying up late chatting with friends and thought leaders of the day. At the end of these long evenings, Neutra would retire to his small bedroom (separate from his wife's *even smaller* bedroom), on the second floor.

Neutra died in 1970 at the age of 78; Dione in 1990 at 90. The ashes of both were scattered in the courtyard.

Address 2300 Silver Lake Boulevard, Los Angeles, CA 90039, www.neutra-vdl.org | Parking Unmetered street parking | Hours Sat 11am–3pm. Guided tours are given; no appointment necessary. Admission: $15 general, $10 students & seniors, free for children under 12. | Tip Walk across Silver Lake Boulevard and take a beautiful stroll on the 2.5-mile path that circles the Silver Lake Reservoir.

103_ The Velaslavasay Panorama

The precursor to motion pictures

In 1787, English painter Robert Barker was walking along a hill absorbing the gorgeous view of Edinburgh when he was struck with inspiration: What would it take to bring this stunning 360-degree sight to everyone? That's how the idea for panoramic art was born. Barker went on to create the first-known full panorama, titled *London from the Roof of Albion Mills*. The goal of the panorama was at least twofold: to immerse viewers so deeply that they should feel transported to a new place or time, blurring their sense of reality, and to expose people to far-flung locales or important moments in history.

Panoramas flourished during the mid to late 19th century in Europe and the United States. Giant domed rotundas in various cities were built to house the artworks, which typically soared upwards of 50 feet and were 400 feet in circumference. Los Angeles exhibited its first panorama in 1887. Its extreme popularity waned after about a year.

The Velaslavasay Panorama is an homage to a now obscure medium, often thought of as a precursor to cinema. It's the only remaining authentic viewing hall in the United States. Visitors walk through a narrow darkened hallway and ascend a spiral staircase (this is all by design, to disorient the eyes and mind), then emerge at eye level with the painting. It's suggested you hang out for at least 15 minutes, which can be a challenge for many fast-paced modern folks. But if you surrender to the experience, the surround sound and lighting can take you far, far away.

The panorama installation is located inside the historic Union Theater, originally a neighborhood movie house projecting newsreels. Behind the building are gardens spilling over with plants and a cooling, meditative fountain. Lots of artsy, fun events are held here, keeping the spirit of independent creativity alive.

Address 1122 W 24th Street, Los Angeles, CA 90007, Tel +1 213.746.2166,
www.panoramaonview.org, panorama@panoramaonview.org | Parking Unmetered street
parking | Hours Fri–Sun noon–6pm | Tip Feast on delicious North African-inspired tacos
at Revolutionario (1436 W Jefferson Boulevard, Suite 70, Los Angeles, CA 90007).

104__ Velveteria

Plush art gets fresh start

We're not just talking kitschy velvet Elvises, although you'll find the King well represented here. Velveteria is a museum dedicated to the art of velvet paintings, 420 of which you'll find on the gallery walls, created by artists from all over the world. It's a respectful and deeply fun curation of a medium that is often derided as the epitome of poor taste.

When cofounder Carl Baldwin was a boy, he would spend weekends visiting his Uncle Charlie in Fullerton. Prior to World War II, Uncle Charlie ended up working with British Petroleum blowing up oil wells in Burma as a tactic to keep the oil out of the hands of the Japanese. During Baldwin's visits, Uncle Charlie, who lost one eye in a Fourth of July firecracker mishap that kept him out of the war, would share tales of his time in Polynesia. Baldwin made his own discovery about his uncle's time abroad when he and his brother found a trove of velvet paintings of naked Polynesian ladies stacked against the back of a closet wall behind Uncle Charlie's Hawaiian shirts.

But Baldwin's passion for velvet paintings truly blossomed when he reunited with a former high-school classmate, Caren Anderson, 30 years after graduating. Together on a trip through Arizona, they acquired a velvet painting of an African-American woman with a blue Afro. This humble purchase begat the legacy that is Velveteria, and a globe-crossing quest to acquire velvet paintings by a range of artists, from the velvet masters like lascivious Edgar Leetag and CeCe Rodriguez to the less recognized painters behind such gems as a Sammy Davis Jesus, velvet unicorns, and the like. Today, Anderson and Baldwin's personal collection includes more than 3,000 pieces.

But the best part of Velveteria, with all due respect to the plush paintings, is engaging with the proprietors. Do not leave the gallery without meeting these skilled raconteurs. Ask about a Leetag, and let it unfold from there.

Address 711 New High Street, Los Angeles, CA 90012, Tel +1 503.309.9299,
www.velveteria.com, velveteriala@gmail.com | **Public transport** .4-mile-walk from
Union Station | **Parking** Metered street parking | **Hours** Wed–Mon 11am–6pm,
closed Tue; $10 admission | **Tip** Eastside Market (1013 Alpine Street, Los Angeles,
CA 90012) is a true Italian deli dating back to 1929, known for its supremely delicious
sandwiches, a local favorite being the hot roast beef and pastrami.

105 _ Venice Art Walls

Where it's okay to spray

Until there was sanctioned graffiti in Los Angeles, alacrity and efficiency were hallmark talents of any street artist who succeeded in getting their work up without being caught for vandalism. Graffiti as art was a new concept for LA in the 1980s and 1990s. It drifted over from New York, where writers had been making so-called subway art since the 1970s.

At "the Pit" in Venice Beach, once a giant expanse of concrete walls, picnic tables, and pavement, graffiti was happening with joyous insouciance because even though spray-painting the walls was illegal, it was unofficially tolerated; the colorful creations suited the edgy, artistic vibe of the neighborhood – that is, until 1999, when almost the entire site was demolished. The fact that any walls still stand is testimony to the devoted passions of local advocates, including In Creative Unity, a graffiti production company, which fought successfully to preserve the Pit's 25-year street-art legacy.

Before the community succeeded in legalizing graffiti on the walls, there was a regulating presence among contributing artists. Established writers could cover more prominent and larger spaces, while the newbies, or "toys," needed to prove themselves as deserving. It was a competitive move to paint over someone else's work. Currently, the walls are managed and curated by the STP Foundation, a nonprofit organization supporting public art. Anyone can graffiti the walls so long as they have a permit and wear it at all times. Permits can be obtained on-site or online through the STP Foundation's website. Minors may not spray, but they can use a paint roller or brush to make their mark.

With toes sunk into warm sand and an unobstructed view of the glorious Pacific Ocean, visitors can be rebellious punks and spray the day away, or just admire the bright and expressive writing on the walls.

Address Just west of 1800 Oceanfront Walk, Venice, CA 90291, Tel +1.818.446.6787, www.veniceartwalls.com, info@stpla.org | Parking Paid beach lots and metered street parking | Hours Sat & Sun, 10am–until 1/2 hour before sunset | Tip Stroll the Venice Canals (located at Carroll Court and Eastern Canal Court, Venice, CA 90293) – their uncanny resemblance to the famous canals of Italy's Venice is quite a treat.

106__Vineland Drive-In
Just like when Grandma and Grandpa were kids

The drive-in is alive and well in the City of Industry! Seven nights a week, rain or shine, Pacific Theatres Vineland Drive-In projects double features on four outdoor screens. Talk all you want in the privacy of your car without being shushed by fellow moviegoers. Discreetly bring your well-behaved canine friend. Crying baby? No problem.

The original theater opened with just one screen, more than 60 years ago, in 1955, with a showing of Disney's *20,000 Leagues Under the Sea*. It's been in operation continuously ever since, with the exception of a dark week after 9/11.

Owning a single-screen drive-in is a recipe for going broke in modern times. To make the business more viable, Pacific Theatres remodeled in 1981, adding three more screens, and now hosts a swap meet during the day. By hook or by crook, the Vineland somehow keeps chugging along.

The snack bar is definitely worth a visit. The lure is not so much the classic movie fare: popcorn, hot dogs, candy, and pizza. Nor is it the clean, well-maintained bathrooms, although that is a bonus. The crowning feature is the old film projector on display and the gigantic metal circular plates that served up the film back in the pre-digital days. The plates revolutionized movie screening by allowing reels of film to be spliced together and held on a round tray before being fed through one projector. No longer did theaters need two projectors per screen to show an uninterrupted film.

Showtimes are when darkness falls. Some audience members like to go old school and turn the truck or wagon around and stretch out in back. Others bring camp chairs to sit outside their car. If movie popcorn is not your thing, feel free to bring your own snacks. A food truck is also known to park on location offering different culinary options, including that old street-fair mainstay: deep-fried funnel cake – with ice cream, no less.

Address 443 N Vineland Avenue, City of Industry, CA 91746, Tel +1 626.961.9262, www.vinelanddriveintheater.com, vinelandd@decurion.com | **Hours** Mon–Thu gates open 6:30pm, Fri–Sun gates open 6:45pm. Screenings begin when darkness falls. Pricing varies by day; check website for details. FM radio is required for audio. | **Tip** Come early and spend time at Bassett Park across the street (510 Vineland Avenue, La Puente, CA 91746). The county park offers a water play area for kids in the hot months.

107__Walt's Barn

Where Mr. Disney's imagination wandered

When Walt Disney and his wife, Lillian, considered buying the house at 355 North Carolwood Drive in swanky, mansion-filled Holmby Hills, they had two priorities. Walt needed space for his cherished miniature trains and Lillian for her beloved garden beds. They agreed on the house, but argued over the same plot of land for their respective hobbies. After some tense negotiations, Lillian won out, but that's because Walt decided to build his railroad *below* his wife's garden instead, creating a 90-foot S-shaped tunnel. The curves allowed for maximum darkness, making for a scarier train ride. That tunnel was just part of the nearly half-mile track Walt built in his backyard. Also included was a 46-foot-long trestle soaring 12 feet high. Atop the track ran his "Carolwood Pacific Railroad," a small-scale live steam train, an eighth the size of the real thing. Passengers straddled the cars, like riding a horse.

Surrounded by the hand-laid tracks sat a red barn modeled after the one Walt loved as a boy on his family's farm in Missouri. Within that barn, Walt ran the track switchboard, and tinkered and imagined. The barn was his respite from the demands of the studio. In fact, he spent so much time sheltered in its cozy one-room space, some believe the barn was where he hatched the idea of creating a giant amusement park.

When Disney's Holmby Hills home was sold, the barn was dismantled and rebuilt in its current location on Zoo Drive. About 80 percent of the structure is original. Inside, you'll find exhibits on the history of railroads and pieces of Walt's personal collection, like the black engine and tender in the middle of the room, ruined on its way to the States from England, where Walt had discovered and fallen in love with it. Of note is the original Carolwood control panel, with which Walt operated his train. In fact, it's the first ride control system of its kind.

Address 5202 Zoo Drive, Los Angeles, CA 90027, Tel +1 310.213.0722, www.carolwood.com/walts-barn | Parking Free on-site lots | Hours Third Sun of the month 11am–3pm | Tip In Griffith Park, just west of Walt's Barn, is the giant Travel Town Museum, where old locomotives and their cars from the 1880s to 1940s rest.

108__West Hollywood Park Tennis Courts

Practice your groundstrokes on a rooftop

Three well-maintained tennis courts rest atop the parking structure next to the West Hollywood Public Library across the street from the big blue Pacific Design Center.

Upsides are abundant: no fee; free two-hour parking with validation; relatively well maintained restrooms; three round cast-concrete tables with benches under a roof awning to provide respite from the sun for your snack or post-game picnic; lighted courts for evening play.

Yet these perks pale next to the rooftop's expansive bird's-eye views. Look north for the amazing Santa Monica Mountains with beautiful hillside estates glittering like gems above the flatlands. Turn to the south for an equally delightful but different cityscape. By golly, it's pretty. And it's a great place to get a workout too, whether you don your finest tennis whites or not-quite-ready-for-Wimbledon gray sweats.

The courts are open daily on a first-come-first-serve basis. And it tends to get pretty busy on the weekends and in the evenings. Arrive early for the best chance of getting to play without a wait. Alternatively, go on a weekday morning or afternoon, when demand is lower.

Access to the courts is via a borrowed key card, which is acquired in the office on the first floor of the parking garage below the tennis courts in exchange for picture ID (a library card won't do). When you return the card and pick up your ID, the parking office will provide validation. Note that there are two parking structures separated by a long driveway. Only one offers validation for the courts: as you enter from North San Vincente Boulevard, the structure on the left is for the tennis courts and neighboring West Hollywood Park. The one on the right is for the library.

The city has plans to add a water play area to the park in the near future. You might never leave.

Address 625 N San Vicente Boulevard, West Hollywood, CA 90069, Tel +1 323.848.6308, www.weho.org (click on "West Hollywood Park Tennis Courts"), recreation@weho.org | Parking Two-hour validated parking in structure below the tennis courts | Hours Daily 7am–9pm | Tip The adjacent West Hollywood Library is awesome. Those great rooftop views are equally fantastic from the floor-to-ceiling windows on the second floor of the north side of the library. Black leather couches add a nice touch.

109 Wildlife Waystation

Lions and tigers and bears

On a spring day, after much needed rain, the hills of Little Tujunga Canyon radiate a bright green from the freshly sprouted grass, and the chaparral looks surprisingly plump. Five miles up the canyon road, just past a tight hairpin turn, live 40 chimpanzees saved from biomedical research labs. Together they make up the largest chimpanzee sanctuary in the western United States.

The chimpanzees are part of a group of 400 rescued animals living at the Wildlife Waystation. Tucked into a valley surrounded by three rolling hills in the western Angeles National Forest, the Wildlife Waystation was incorporated in 1976, when founder Martine Colette bought the 162-acre property. Injured wild animals come to the Wildlife Waystation to heal and, when possible, return to their natural habitats. But a fair share of exotics, like Drifter the tiger, are at the sanctuary because they were improperly acquired as pets. Unfortunately, vulnerability due to domestication means that many of the exotic animals can no longer be expected to survive in the wild. At the Wildlife Waystation, a staff of 34 and a volunteer team of 400 lovingly work to give these animals the best lives possible through high-quality care and compassion.

You can visit the refuge as a guest of its founder, wildlife expert Martine Colette, who offers bimonthly private luncheons and dinners in the beautifully appointed garden courtyard of her home next to the grounds. The safari party comes with a tour of the property and an introduction to some of the animals. As patrons dine under the giant canopy, glassware glistening in the candlelight, they can hear the critters bray, roar, and call. Funds raised through these events help support the caretaking costs of the animals.

Another way to experience the Wildlife Waystation is by volunteering. Volunteer orientations are held the second Saturday of each month from 9am to noon. Reserve a spot in advance.

Address 14831 Little Tujunga Canyon Road, Sylmar, CA 91342, Tel +1 818.899.5201,
www.wildlifewaystation.org, info@wildlifewaystation.org | Parking Free on-site lot |
Hours Gift shop: 9am–5pm. Lunch and dinner safari parties by reservation only, costs are
$100–$250 per person, depending on event. Visitors to the Wildlife Waystation must be
at least 18 years of age. | Tip Ranch Side Cafe (11355 Foothill Boulevard, Sylmar,
CA 91342), at the base of Little Tujunga Canyon, offers non-chain breakfast options,
burgers, and, surprisingly, Ethiopian food.

110__The Wishing Well
A symbol of renewal

Elegantly dressed, internationally known Chinese movie star Anna May Wong wielded a hefty shovel as she planted a willow tree. It was 1938, and the occasion was the inauguration of the Wishing Well fountain. It's said to be a miniature replica of Seven Star Cavern, a Yosemite-like wonderland, full of watery caves, rivers, lakes and craggy mountainsides. Designed by Henry Hong K. Liu, a professor at USC, it was once a formidable art structure that has taken a beating over the decades.

Many Angelenos avoided the original Chinatown in the late 19th century. It was perceived as unhealthy and dangerous. The streets were narrow and cramped, the buildings ramshackle and dimly lit. But, there were other cultural issues at play. The Chinese Exclusion Acts of the 1880s created an institutionalized racism aimed at keeping the Chinese out of the United States. Chinese laborers were seen as competition to those who were American-born – even though Chinese immigrants were relied upon heavily just 30 years prior to build US railroads. Chinese women were at the railyards too – in hideous conditions and trapped as prostitutes. Race covenants kicked in during the early part of the 20th century. Real-estate advertisements often stated, "Whites only." The presence of nonwhite residents was thought to bring property values down.

It was this climate in which the Wishing Well was made. Old Chinatown had been razed, making way for Union Station and the 101 freeway. Seizing an opportunity to redefine their identity, a group of Chinese pooled their money to build the Central Plaza, a colorful outdoor retail space featuring the fountain. Nature was worshipped in classical Chinese art, and the fountain's purpose was to be a beacon of peace and contemplation in the urban world. The new Chinatown quickly became a vibrant destination for all races and ethnicities.

Address On Gin Ling Way in the middle of the Central Plaza, 950 N Broadway Los Angeles, CA 90012 | Public transport Metro Gold Line to the Chinatown Station, then a .5-mile walk | Parking Metered street parking | Hours Always viewable | Tip Check out the mural *Chinese Celestial Dragon*, painted by Tyrus Wong, located in the Central Plaza, at the corner of Broadway and Bamboo. Wong was one of the first Chinese Americans employed by Walt Disney Studios; his artistic style was the basis for the animated feature *Bambi*.

111_ York Boulevard

The coolest shopping street you've never heard of

York Boulevard in Highland Park offers up an LA retail experience that its trendier counterparts like Robertson Boulevard and Montana Avenue do not. Once the hub of Los Angeles's Arts and Crafts movement, the surrounding neighborhood saw an influx of Mexican Americans in the 1960s, followed by a wave of post-millennium gentrification. Today, it reflects a cross-section of LA, a mash-up of cultures and ethnicities where you'll find tattooed dads pushing strollers and hipsters sporting the latest trends alongside Latino locals who have lived in the neighborhood for decades. Here, a funky mom-and-pop discount store shares the same block with a specialty boutique pedaling pricey vintage typewriters. It's a clash of old and new, wealthy-ish and working class – all fiercely independent.

Between Avenues 50 and 52, York is packed with shops and eateries. You could easily occupy yourself for an entire day on this two-block strip alone. Start off with a perfect shot of espresso from the gourmet Café de Leche, then browse books next door at Pop-Hop and wander through the various vintage clothing shops. For lunch, stop into the crowded Jugos Azteca, a fresh juice and tortas joint. If your sweet tooth calls, indulge in a cone at Scoops, an artisanal ice-cream shop. Take it with you while you browse vintage vinyl at Permanent Records. Grab a slice at Town Pizza for dinner, then hit Hermosillo for a pint of craft beer. Cap off the evening with a rock show at Hi Hat, which often features local bands.

Refreshingly devoid of glamour and glitz, York's lack of landscaping and no-frills architecture simply add to its urban charm. But as you might expect of Los Angeles, it's not totally free of celebrity. Marc Maron, the host of the extremely popular podcast "WTF with Marc Maron" is recorded at Maron's home in Highland Park. He might be the biggest quasi-celebrity sighting you'll experience on York – and that's a good thing.

Address York Boulevard between Avenue 50 and Avenue 52, Los Angeles, CA 90042 | Parking Paid lots; metered and unmetered street parking | Hours Opening times vary from shop to shop; most shops closed Mondays | Tip Be sure to step into Shorthand (5028 York Boulevard, Los Angeles, CA 90042), a fancy stationery store with two gorgeous vintage letterpresses – both well over 100 years old.

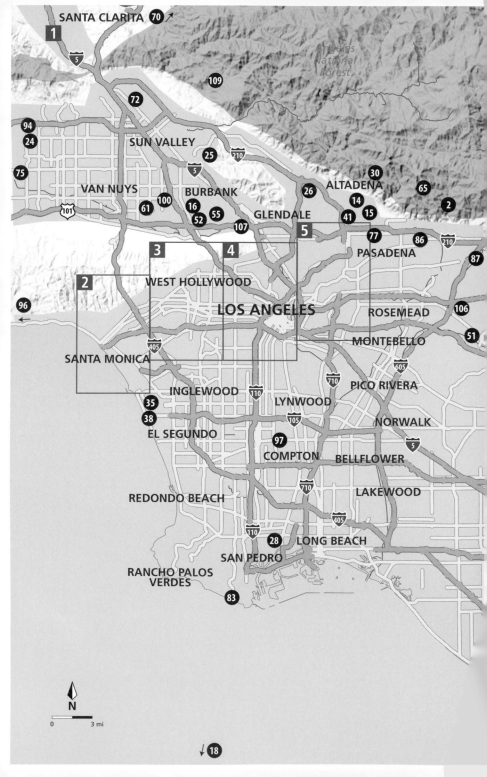

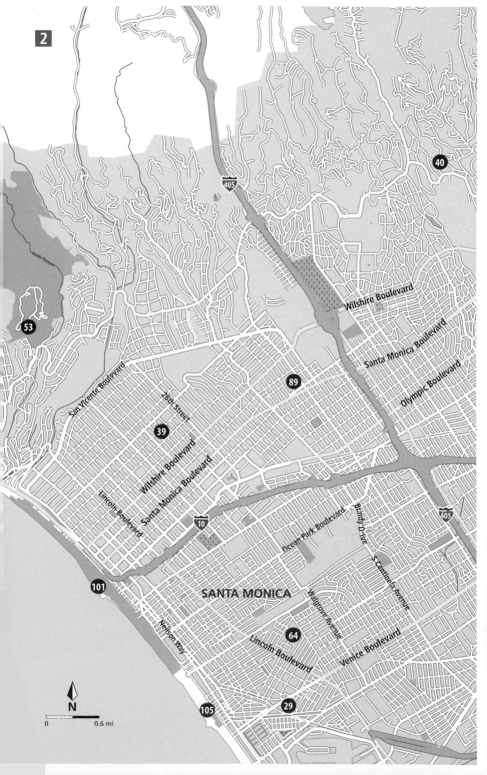

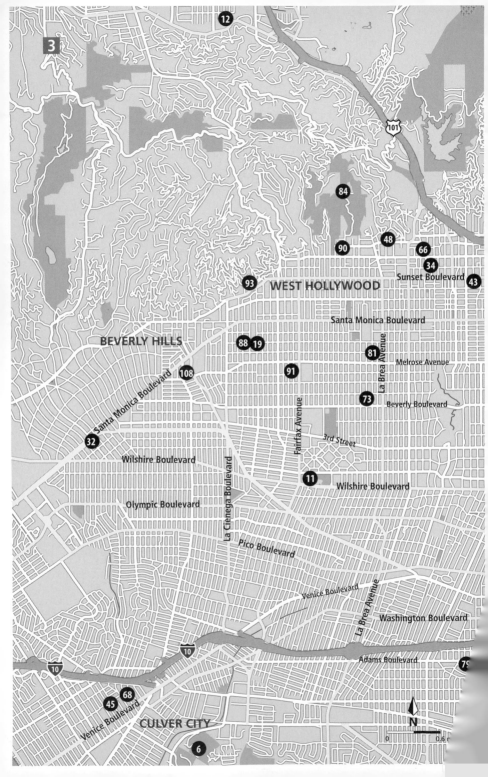

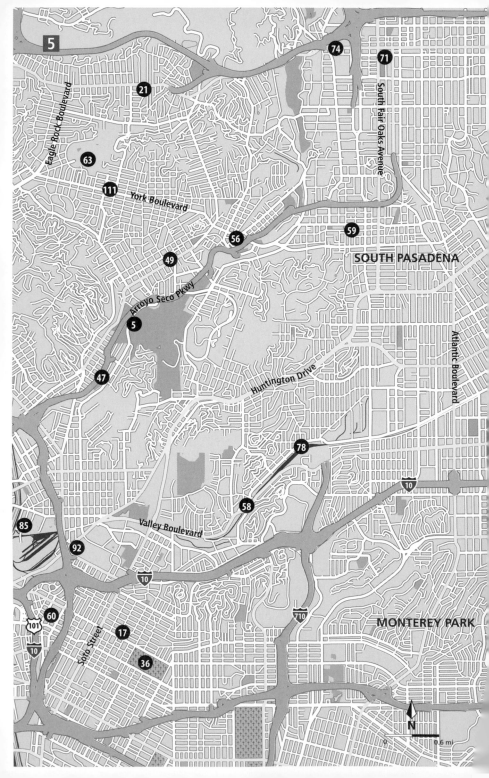

Lucia Jay von Seldeneck,
Carolin Huder, Verena Eidel
**111 PLACES IN BERLIN
THAT YOU SHOULDN'T MISS**
ISBN 978-3-95451-208-9

Rüdiger Liedtke
**111 PLACES IN MUNICH
THAT YOU SHOULDN'T MISS**
ISBN 978-3-95451-222-5

Frank McNally
**111 PLACES IN DUBLIN
THAT YOU MUST NOT MISS**
ISBN 978-3-95451-649-0

Rike Wolf
**111 PLACES IN HAMBURG
THAT YOU SHOULDN'T MISS**
ISBN 978-3-95451-234-8

Paul Kohl
**111 PLACES IN BERLIN
ON THE TRAIL OF THE NAZIS**
ISBN 978-3-95451-323-9

Peter Eickhoff
**111 PLACES IN VIENNA
THAT YOU SHOULDN'T MISS**
ISBN 978-3-95451-206-5

Sharon Fernandes
**111 PLACES IN NEW DELHI
THAT YOU MUST NOT MISS**
ISBN 978-3-95451-648-3

Sally Asher, Michael Murphy
**111 PLACES IN NEW ORLEANS
THAT YOU MUST NOT MISS**
ISBN 978-3-95451-645-2

Gordon Streisand
**111 PLACES IN MIAMI
AND THE KEYS
THAT YOU MUST NOT MISS**
ISBN 978-3-95451-644-5

Gerd Wolfgang Sievers
111 PLACES IN VENICE
THAT YOU MUST NOT MISS
ISBN 978-3-95451-460-1

Petra Sophia Zimmermann
111 PLACES IN VERONA
AND LAKE GARDA THAT
YOU MUST NOT MISS
ISBN 978-3-95451-611-7

Rüdiger Liedtke,
Laszlo Trankovits
111 PLACES IN CAPE TOWN
THAT YOU MUST NOT MISS
ISBN 978-3-95451-610-0

Annett Klingner
111 PLACES IN ROME
THAT YOU MUST NOT MISS
ISBN 978-3-95451-469-4

Jo-Anne Elikann
111 PLACES IN NEW YORK
THAT YOU MUST NOT MISS
ISBN 978-3-95451-052-8

Giulia Castelli Gattinara,
Mario Verin
111 PLACES IN MILAN
THAT YOU MUST NOT MISS
ISBN 978-3-95451-331-4

Marcus X. Schmid
111 PLACES IN ISTANBUL
THAT YOU MUST NOT MISS
ISBN 978-3-95451-423-6

Floriana Petersen, Steve Werney
111 PLACES IN SAN FRANCISCO
THAT YOU MUST NOT MISS
ISBN 978-3-95451-609-4

John Sykes
111 PLACES IN LONDON
THAT YOU SHOULDN'T MISS
ISBN 978-3-95451-346-8

Acknowledgments

Deep appreciation and respect to the entire team at Emons that helped make this book. Special thanks to our editor, Katrina Fried – patient, diligent, intelligent, and caring, she made our text so much better; Ellen Leach, for her keen copyediting skills and thorough research; and Lyudmila Zotova, our talented photographer, for her good nature and gorgeous images. A big shout out to our friends who drove across town in the thick of traffic for the bonfire photoshoot. To our husbands, Dean and Eric, and children, Izak, Pax, Owen, Emmet, thank you for supporting us with meals and ideas while we stayed up late to write, and missed bedtimes. To the countless number of people we interviewed, that helped us flesh out the complex and colorful stories that make Los Angeles so special, your time and knowledge gave this book the details and nuances we sought.

L.M. & J.P.

Authors

Laurel Moglen has produced news for local NPR affiliates KPCC and KCRW, including the programs "Which Way LA?" and "AirTalk," where she was immersed in all things Los Angeles – its politics, history, current events, and cultural vastness. She makes podcasts too, including one for Travelocity covering what to do, see, and eat in cities around the world. Travel and discovering the subtleties of what gives a place its identity is a passion of hers, and nowhere is it more fascinating, complicated, and mercurial than in Los Angeles, her home for many years.

Julia Posey is a writer, artist, and clothing designer. She is a native Angeleno and has worked for NPR affiliate KPCC's "AirTalk" and "Talk of the City." She has also written and filed stories for KPCC news. She has held many jobs, and in her inauspicious youth – she even worked in a recycling truck. She lives in Highland Park with her husband, sons, and sweet dog.

Photographer

Lyudmila Zotova's photographs have been featured in the *Wall Street Journal,* Yahoo News, and Eater National, and she is the photographer of the book *111 Shops in Los Angeles That You Must Not Miss* (Emons, 2015). Zotova is an alumnus of The Art Institute of California-Orange County and resides in San Diego, California.